Grandparents
COLORADO STYLE

by Mike Link and Kate Crowley

Adventure Publications, Inc.
Cambridge, Minnesota

Dedication:

Matthew, Aren, Ryan, and Annalise, you are the real stars of our books.

Photo credits:

Cover photos courtesy of Mike Link and Kate Crowley.

All photos are copyright Mike Link and Kate Crowley unless otherwise noted.

Dragon Boat Festival photo courtesy of Kit Williams/Colorado Dragon Boat Festival.

Cover and book design by Jonathan Norberg
10 9 8 7 6 5 4 3 2 1
Copyright 2009 by Mike Link and Kate Crowley
Published by Adventure Publications, Inc.
820 Cleveland St. S
Cambridge, MN 55008
1-800-678-7006
www.adventurepublications.net
All rights reserved
Printed in China
ISBN-13: 978-1-59193-227-7
ISBN-10: 1-59193-227-0

Contents

Introduction

Grandparents Colorado Style is for today's grandparents who want to spend more time discovering the world with their grandchildren. This book is about opportunities for adults and children to have fun, laugh and share. Of course, Colorado is ripe with more possibilities than we can cover, but this is a place to get started. We decided to write this book because of our experiences with our grandchildren—three boys and a girl. They provide us with a lot of fun, but we also have a responsibility to them. We can use our time together to help them learn and grow as individuals.

In writing this book we've had to stop and think about the knowledge we've gained, how we learned valuable life lessons and how we could pass our wisdom to our grandchildren. With the changing times, we found that several experiences have become endangered—solitude, silence, open space, dark night skies, free time, reading books and home-cooked food.

Consider the following changes:

1. Farms are no longer a part of most children's experiences. In 1900, farmers accounted for forty percent of our census. By 1990, the total fell below two percent.

2. Open space was once a playground. Now it is slated for development. Children are left with only fenced yards and indoor locations.

3. The "out in the country" experience is disappearing. Urban sprawl means an hour's drive from the inner city to any country areas.

4. Tree climbing is more difficult now. There are few open areas of trees for Jacks and Jills to climb magic beanstalks.

5. The chance to be bored—which is an opportunity to be creative—isn't often in the schedule. Children are signed up for every organized activity and training available, eliminating family time and free time.

6. Sports used to be for fun. Now some parents have children choose a sport, then send them to summer camps where winning is what matters.

7. Canning, pickling and baking—all of those wonderful activities that filled the root-cellars and pantries of the past—are less common.

Today's world has seen some bad and dangerous trends. Fast food (and obesity) is the norm. Meth and other deadly drugs flood our cities, our neighborhoods and our schools.

Fortunately, our grandchildren have us. The role of the grandparent can be different than it was when we were kids, and we can adapt, too. Grandparents have many opportunities:

1. Grandparents are living longer than ever before and can influence their grandchildren longer.

2. Parents work long days, filled with busy hours.

3. Grandparents can provide children with quiet times, new experiences and more play.

4. Grandparents can help introduce children to healthy food; we have the time to prepare it and present it.

5. Children may gain from perspectives other than those of their peers and they may benefit from our guidance and insight.

We may be able to involve the extended family in more activities and be part of the new modern family of the twenty-first century.

That's not to say we should take on the role of mother and father. Instead our place is to supplement a child's parents, to help them wherever our help is wanted and needed. Let's use the time we have with our grandchildren to instill in them important values, to teach them about the world around them and to help shape them into better people.

A Word from Mike Link

"Where are you dad?"

"We got a late start and have about an hour till we get to you, why?"

"Well you better hurry. Your grandson heard Gampa was coming and now we're sitting out on the curb waiting for you to arrive."

An hour later we found our greeting party on the curb, on the blanket. Who could ask for a better welcome than that? That's the love our grandchildren have for us if we are willing to involve ourselves in their lives. Our greatest gift to them is our love and attention; they are the greatest gift we could receive. We watch all four of our grandchildren grow; Annalise is now past her first birthday so we are starting the cycle over. The twins (age 4), Aren and Ryan, are fighting the loneliness of having their father in Afghanistan and trying to get all the "man attention" they can from grandpa. (Each twin is engaged in the other's life and a defender of "my brother," yet each is separate in more than looks.) Matthew is five and beginning to look like a young boy rather than a little kid. The passion for Thomas the Train is now gone; pirates and "guys"—any little plastic figure of a person—dominate play now. We need to be mentors, guides, and trustworthy companions for the children.

The role of the grandparent is significant, and played an important part in Kate's life, my life, and those of our children. I spent all my "non-school" time living with my grandparents in Rice Lake, Wisconsin, while my father worked evenings and weekends to try to get us out of the poverty that surrounded us. It was not a desertion of responsibility, but rather a type of sharing. I was born in Rice Lake, where my grandparents would live until their deaths.

My dad worked second shift, from three p.m. to midnight, and that meant we had little time together, so my grandfather taught me to play catch, to drive, to work. He was my partner. My grandmother picked berries with me, taught me the pleasure of fresh baked pies and cookies. She was the stern partner who could laugh, but I saw her more as the person who ran the home. My second set of grandparents were in the same town and I remember the kolaches that my grandmother made, the canary in the living room, but not much more since they were not the type to play and share warmth with me.

I was also lucky to know my great-grandparents and to see my heritage through this multi-level set of grandparents. It was a wonderful way to connect time and generations. My great-great-grandmother, Ogima Benisi Kwe (Chief Bird Woman) was from the La Court O'Reilles reservation and she married my great-great-grandfather John Quaderer who was from Liechtenstein.

Their daughter, Anna Kahl, my great-grandmother, was a wonderful woman who raised not only her 13 children on their farm, but also raised five of my uncles who would move back to the reservation as they reached adulthood. She carried forward the tradition that a grandparent should be the role model and the teacher, while the parents provide safety, home, food, and provisions. I will always remember her in her polka dot dress and brimmed hat. She loved her hat and when her daughters threatened to throw it away, she cut off the brim and pretended it was a new hat that, therefore, could not be thrown out. She is part of who I am. My Anishanabe heritage created the succession of grandparent/grandchild roles and bonds that continues today. I believe that the extended role of the traditional grandparent is one that fits the needs of today.

My parents stepped forward to provide support and love for my children and took them traveling, let them try things that they had to do to learn and grow. Most of all, my children knew they loved them.

Now we have our grandchildren living in two states. Matthew is closest to us, one hundred miles away, and lives where we travel regularly. This gives us the benefit of regular short visits, a few weekends, and a few travel weeks. This is a great mix, one that allows us to jump in, have a great time and leave, but not to spoil him.

We want to support our children and our grandchildren and we take our own admonition seriously, "be a companion, not a checkbook, be supportive, not a chauffeur." I cannot tell you what presents my grandparents gave me, but I do know about the things we did together. If you want to build those memories get going, take those grandchildren and experience the world again for the first time through their curiosity.

We are pleased to write about Colorado where three of our grandchildren were born. Visiting them in Colorado Springs while their father taught at the Air Force Academy, we had a chance to explore many wonderful places that are in this book. Then they moved to Cheyenne, and we were able to take them with us, to stay in a motel, and hear them say, "Where are we going today, Grandpa?"

We are the elders; we are the starting point for more generations. A Lakota friend told me that growing old does not make you an elder. Be yourself. Be honest, be fun, be open. Grandchildren are gifts from the future—they connect us to their world, and we in turn owe them a connection to ours.

A Word from Kate Crowley

Most of us, if we're lucky, have known our grandparents. We are even luckier if those grandparents lived nearby and enriched our lives. Until the last 50 years, elders have been integral and respected members of our communities. They transported the stories, the history of the people. They were revered and children spent time in their company. The Industrial Revolution, while it has brought us lives of relative ease and abundance, has also brought about the gradual decline of the close-knit, extended family.

Much of the knowledge that the elders and grandparents carried was tied to life on the land. Older grandparents, and those of the generation who are just now becoming grandparents, are the last generation where a majority can remember a time when grandparents lived on farms or in small towns. We can recall the easy, simple times spent with these adults who indulged us; we can share memories with a generation being born into a century with untold opportunities and unfortunately, too many uncertainties.

By the time I was born, I only had two living grandmothers. One lived in California and I have very fuzzy memories of her. My other grandmother lived just a block away from our house and though her Germanic heritage didn't incline her toward a warm, cuddly exterior, I had over 20 years of close acquaintance with her. I even lived with her for four years during and after high school. She was a working woman into her 80s—ironing clothes for people and caring for one or two elderly people in her home, so she didn't have the time or personality to get down on the floor and play with us. But her house was always open to us and we wore a path through our neighbors' backyards to get there. She had a few old toys and books for us to play with and a big old piano, but mostly we came to visit and if we were lucky, on a hot summer day, she'd make us a root beer float.

A Sunday ritual for the first 16 years of my life was dinner at "Ma's"as we called her: roasted chicken, mashed potatoes and gravy, cooked corn, cabbage salad, and either apple or custard pie. I only have to think about it and I'm coming through her front door into a room moist with the steam of cooked vegetables.

Our most firmly held memories of time spent with our grandparents are tied to our senses. These are the things that will stay with children as they grow to adulthood and recall their times spent with their grandparents. That, and laughter.

One of the most mouth-watering memories I have is a summer day picking tomatoes with my grandmother. It was a hot day and the sun was beating down on us as we moved through the pungent rows of tomato plants. I must have been old enough to be considered trustworthy—she expected me to pick the right ones and handle them properly. What do I remember most about that day? That she packed cheese sandwiches (probably Velveeta) and I have never eaten anything more delicious than a rich, sweet tomato right off the vine, still holding the sun's heat, with juice running down my chin, followed by a bite of soft cheese on white bread. The smells and tastes flowed together and I can still see us, joined together by the simple act of harvesting our food.

I have waited a very long time to become a grandmother and not just because our daughters chose to wait until their 30s to have children. Even when my two children were still pre-teens, I was contemplating grandparenthood. I changed my first name from Kathy to Kate because I couldn't picture a "grandma Kathy." I packed away all the Fisher Price toys in their original boxes to share with the next generation and saved as many of their books as possible. I enjoyed raising my two children and I knew I wanted to have similar experiences again, but without the worries and day-to-day concerns that accompany young parenthood. I knew even then, that as a grandparent I would be able to have fun, play with the kids, act silly, share what I've learned in life with them, but have the luxury of going home at the end of the day to a quiet, clean house.

Now we have three grandsons—all arrived in the span of one year, and a granddaughter to counterbalance all that testosterone, and we are looking forward to years of adventures together. Matthew, Ryan, Aren and Annalise are more precious to me than I could've imagined, just as I know your grandchildren are for you. We are not reliving our childhood through them, as some might think, we are participating in their journey into the future—a future we can only imagine. And we want our journey together to be as much fun and full of learning and discovery as possible. This is why we have written this book—this Field Guide—to help other grandparents find those unique and unforgettable places that will combine fun and facts, history and humor, excitement and enduring memories for you and the special children in your lives.

How to Use This Book

The suggestions in this book are just suggestions. Some experiences are unmatchable anywhere else in the state. Others can be replicated. If you are not near the museum, park or site we highlight, find a similar place near you. Read our suggestions and pay special attention to "Bonding and bridging" to tie your visit to a life lesson.

We do not advocate that you become the "wallet" or the "chauffeur." Consider an active participation in friendship and sharing that is enriched by love. We want you to receive the respect due an elder, to share your experience and to enjoy the love that can flow between generations.

One of the themes of this book is that things change. This is true for everything, including the state's attractions. They sometimes close, renovate or move. When in doubt, *CALL BEFORE YOU LEAVE HOME.*

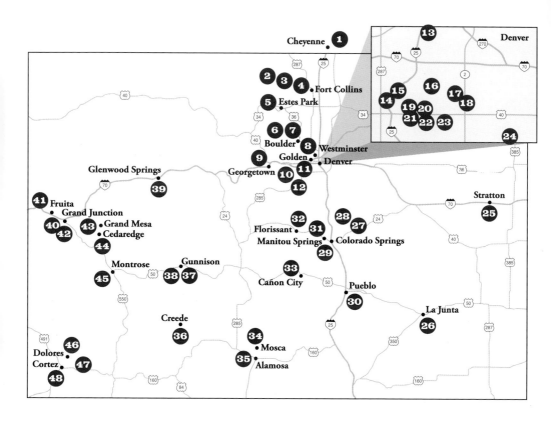

Cheyenne **1**

2 **3** **4** Fort Collins

5 Estes Park

6 **7**

Boulder **8**

9 Golden Westminster

11 Denver

Georgetown **10**

12

Glenwood Springs

39

41 Fruita

Grand Junction

40 **43** Grand Mesa

42 Cedaredge

44

Montrose Gunnison

45 **38** **37**

Florissant **32** **31**

Manitou Springs **28** **27**

29 Colorado Springs

33

Cañon City Pueblo

30

Creede **36**

34 Mosca

35 Alamosa

Dolores **46**

Cortez **47**

48

Stratton

25

13 Denver

15 **16** **17**

14 **19** **20** **18**

21 **22** **23**

24

La Junta

26

The sites appear in the book in the order below, beginning with those in the northern part of the state, proceeding south and then to the west.

Frontier Days

Is it possible to invite Coloradoans to cross the border and slip to the north for a celebration that has no peer? Cheyenne hosts "Frontier Days," the rodeo and western celebration that defines what "out west" really means. It is so popular that the attendance is more than the population of Wyoming, so Colorado must be well represented. So come north of the Colorado border and let go with a few whoops and hollers, a cowboy hat, kerchief, blue jeans, and cowboy boots. The event is built around the rodeo, "The Daddy of them

All" according to a 1919 newspaper article. It is still a large rodeo, with over "40 bucking bulls and 70 saddle and bareback broncs in each performance." Bareback bronc riding and bull riding on a 2,000 pound animal is colorful and dramatic. Steer wrestling is exciting, but you must also question why a person would leap from a charging horse onto this large and dangerous animal—maybe bulldogging is a better name since it is a little like trying to catch a runaway bulldozer.

Barrel racing is fast and the women who do this are outstanding riders who can really show their skill in this arena. In contrast to this coordination and speed between rider and mount, there is the wild horse race; an event as chaotic as any "organized" event can be with a half-dozen teams of three trying to saddle and ride an unbroken horse around the track.

The Grand Parade is a great favorite for the family with more horses than any other parade we know of. The history of the parade might have begun with wild cowboys riding their charging broncs through the streets with their six guns blazing, but today it is organized and so family-friendly that it is repeated four times a week and you need to stake out a good spot!

There is a Midway, but that is not where we took our grandchildren. Instead you will want to visit the air show and watch the parachutists, observe the planes, and find a place to watch the Thunderbirds in their precision aerobatics. As military life and cowboy life mix together in this citywide event, it combines the diverse elements of eastern Wyoming and provides a setting for families to learn, observe and participate.

Bonding and bridging:

Pancakes. That is the key to a cowboy and a grandchild breakfast. What grandparent (I really am thinking about grandfathers) does not make an occasional pancake with their own secret recipe and ingredients? The grandchildren can help stir; if it is safe and the kids are old enough they might flip, and ultimately with maple syrup, enjoy. This becomes a family tradition and a highlight of visits.

Cheyenne has taken this another step with the largest pancake feed we have ever seen. It is massive. The line stretches out for blocks and it seems like you will wait forever, but that line just keeps moving and you keep visiting and the anticipation keeps growing and suddenly you can see the pancakes coming out of the mobile kitchen. You might even see the cakes flipping in the air before landing on a plate held by a Boy Scout who tries to satisfy the hungry people.

There is music, the downtown setting, and lots of people enjoying a communal meal of flapjacks that will reinforce how important food and shared meals are to your relationship.

A word to the wise:

There are events in the Oasis area and in Wild Horse Gulch, plus a behind-the-chutes tour of the animals (who are the real stars of the week long event), but sometimes the events, the crowds, and the noise can get to be too much and the constant stimulus can wear out grandparents and grandchildren alike. The escape route is across the road. The Arboretum, picnic grounds, and playgrounds of Lions Park are the place to find solitude, have a snack, play quietly, or just walk and relax.

Age of grandchild: all

Best season: Summer

Contact: Frontier Park, Cheyenne, WY • www.cfdrodeo.com

Also check out:

Range Call Rodeo, Meeker: www.meekercolorado.com/rangecall.htm

Rooftop Rodeo, Estes Park: estesparkcvb.com/events.cfm

Collegiate Peaks Stampede Rodeo, Buena Vista: www.buenavistacolorado.org/index.htm

Flying Heels Rodeo Series, Granby: www.vacationsinc.com/rodeo.htm

Adopt the pace of nature: her secret is patience. RALPH WALDO EMERSON

The Farm at Lee Martinez Park

Nowadays, very few children have the opportunity to experience life on the farm, unlike their grandparents who grew up on one or spent summers on relatives' farms. Statistically, the change is enormous. In 1900, half of the U.S. population lived on farms and today that number is less than two percent and still falling. It is critical that our grandchildren understand our connection to and dependence on farmers and farm animals.

The Farm at Lee Martinez Park won't look exactly like the farms you knew as a child, but it still has the same silo, barn and chicken house that the Nelson family used when this was an operating dairy farm in the 1920s and '30s. In many ways, it more closely resembles a petting zoo, and so it is the younger grandchild who will enjoy the visit the most.

There are chickens, goats, sheep, pigs, cows and ponies to pet and feed. You can purchase a scoop of oats from the Farm Store and there is hardly anything kids enjoy more than feeding animals. The small Farm Heritage Museum will interest the grandparent more that the grandchild, since its displays old implements, toy tractors and products from earlier eras. Your grandchildren will race through this space and you will find them near the door trying to hoist a real bale of hay, using the pulley system.

The Chicken Coop will fascinate them since they can see the boxes where the eggs are laid and parked outside there is a real Farmall tractor that they can climb on and even turn the steering wheel.

Most of the time, the cows are outside, but you might find a cow in the stanchion being milked. The kids will also enjoy the silo, with its echo chamber. Curious about how much water a cow requires to make a gallon of milk daily? See the display about milk production.

One of the most popular parts of this Farm is the pony ride. What child can resist? You purchase tickets at the Farm Store and in order to ride, one adult must lead them around the fenced arena for 15 minutes.

Bonding and bridging:

All animals are fascinating to kids, whether the animals are domestic or exotic. A visit to the Farm opens up many opportunities for shared discoveries and observations. What does the sheep's wool feel like, how many eggs are in the chicken's nest and what color are they? The pigs really do seem to like to be in the mud, why? Whether you had farm experience as a child or not, you can still share an appreciation of these animals, along with your grandchild. We can also ask if the animals look happy in their pens. While we don't think it's a good idea to give them human emotions, we can talk about ways to treat them humanely. This farm is similar to the farms of the early twentieth century, with small herds of livestock and flocks of free ranging chickens that fed the family throughout the year.

A word to the wise:

Like most year-round facilities for kids, The Farm features a variety of special events, many related to holidays. In the fall, there are events for Halloween and pumpkin picking, the December holidays feature a brunch with Santa, and in the summer there is a stick horse rodeo, an annual fundraiser to adopt an animal, and tractor races, to name just a few. You can find out what's coming up by reading *the Recreator*, which comes out three times a year. Pick it up at recreation facilities and libraries—or in the Ft. Collins newspaper!

Age of grandchild: 2 to 10

Best season: Spring, Summer, Fall

Contact: 600 N Sherwood, Fort Collins, CO 80521 • (970) 221-6665 • www.fcgov.com/thefarm

Also check out:

Cross Orchards Historic Farm, Grand Junction:
www.wcmuseum.org/crossorchards.htm

Plumb Farm Learning Center, Greeley:
www.greeleygov.com/Museums/PlumbFarm.aspx

Rocky Mountain Institute, Almont: www.roundmountain.org

Sunflower Farm, Longmont: www.sunflowerfarminfo.com

The Urban Farm, Stapleton: www.theurbanfarm.org

If a child is to keep alive his inborn sense of wonder, he needs the companionship of at least one adult who can share it, rediscovering with him the joy, excitement and mystery of the world we live in. RACHEL CARSON

Science Discovery Center

Remember the image of the mad scientist? Grandparents probably remember the parody of Albert Einstein, the wild-haired, absent-minded, one-tracked person who represented the scientists of the fifties and sixties. Today that scientist has been replaced with the adventurous biologist roaming the rain forests and the jungles, or the white-coated technicians banging away on the keyboard and finding strings and the background noise of the Big Bang.

We have probed our world and our universe and through these tests and observations we have unlocked amazing experiences and unbelievable elements that used to be confined to wizards and magicians.

In this wonderful Science Center, children sample both physical and biological science with activities that will fill their minds with the key questions—what if, how about, what would happen if? This is inquiry, the building of minds that will seek answers and solutions throughout their lives.

Imagine a tennis-ball race where different angles and pathways test gravity; or think about sitting in a chair and grabbing a line that runs through pulleys to raise yourself toward the ceiling. Or think of this scenario: A blower keeps balls suspended, but what if you broke the flow with your arm or hand? Do your grandchildren wonder about seat belts? Then a little experiment with Crash Collins will make the point without you having to say a word.

There are microscopes and telescopes to see the universe with different perspectives. A live animal room connects us with our interspecies friends and insects always present us with new forms of life, while mirrors challenge our idea of what the world and our bodies look like. If animals are your favorite, the Colorado room helps connect with the state's natural abundance. Or go back in time and let dinosaurs teach you about life.

Then you can play with lights and electricity. The colored shadow, light tables, shadow wall, and laser patterns are just a few visual delights. And electricity is filled with safe hands-on experiments that will provide you with both amazement and knowledge. This is science at its best and a great inspiration for a life of learning.

Bonding and bridging:

When learning is required, we tend to respond negatively, but if we are engaged in an activity that inspires us, we learn in spite of ourselves. The trick is to let things happen naturally. Grandparents have a special way of becoming mentors for children. Our sharing of experience and wisdom helps the children succeed.

Sometimes we bond by teaching children subtle skills like pacing. Pacing is not something kids are good at, and kids tend to want everything right now. Set the pace through planning before you arrive. How much time you will spend, which exhibits will you go to? When will you leave? Don't try to see everything or read everything. Demonstrate that if you say you will come back—you do. Let them know that you need to sit down, take a food break, sit and talk about what you have seen and what you will see. Don't fall into the trap of doing TOO MUCH!

A word to the wise:

Science is part of everything we do and we can relate the lessons we learn here to the playground. The slide is an inclined plane and we can race balls of different weights and sizes and ask if a big child or a little child will get down the slide faster. Friction is the force that works against you and the objects that slide down. The swing is a pendulum. Swing it by itself and ask why it slows down and stops. The seesaw is a lever. What would happen if the board were moved off center? On the circular merry-go-round we encounter centrifugal force. Who knew that fun was so scientific?

Age of grandchild: 3 and up

Best season: whenever you want a quality indoor experience.

Contact: 703 E. Prospect Road, Fort Collins, CO 80525 • (970) 472-3990
• www.dcsm.org

Also check out:

Denver Museum of Nature and Science: www.dmns.org

Fiske Planetarium and Science Center: www.fiske.colorado.edu

Physics on the playground:
http://content.scholastic.com/browse/article.jsp?id=3615

Western Colorado Math & Science Center: www.sithok.org

To our children we give two things: one is roots, the other wings. ANDY ROONEY

Swetsville Zoo

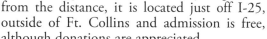

While we were doing research for this book, several people told us we should visit The Swetsville Zoo. We had seen and read the two color brochure and weren't convinced that it was a place that would impress grandchildren. We admit now that we were wrong and that the old adage "Don't Judge a Book by Its Cover" is still true. When we finally stopped at this funky, quirky, unique sculpture garden, we discovered that it was a treat for young children, the old (us) and our 35-year old daughter. Looking a lot like a metal recycling center from the distance, it is located just off I-25, outside of Ft. Collins and admission is free, although donations are appreciated.

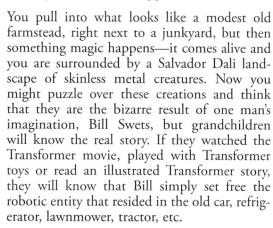

You pull into what looks like a modest old farmstead, right next to a junkyard, but then something magic happens—it comes alive and you are surrounded by a Salvador Dali landscape of skinless metal creatures. Now you might puzzle over these creations and think that they are the bizarre result of one man's imagination, Bill Swets, but grandchildren will know the real story. If they watched the Transformer movie, played with Transformer toys or read an illustrated Transformer story, they will know that Bill simply set free the robotic entity that resided in the old car, refrigerator, lawnmower, tractor, etc.

Here recycling takes on a completely new shape and meaning. Almost any piece of metal that saw service in a previous mechanical life can be found incorporated into these fantastical and funny creatures. What the kids most enjoy are the dinosaur-like visages and shapes—some even the same size as the skeletons standing in museums. Grandparents will smile and chuckle at the whimsical and tongue-in-cheek names given to the creatures. Some of the pieces move with the wind, but most of the 150 sculptures are stationary, turning darker shades of rust as time and weather take their toll. Near the parking lot there are sculptures on display that are for sale, created by other artists. There is also a Museum filled with antique machines and oddities, including a bicycle with 10 seats. You won't spend much more than an hour at this Sculpture Park, but you will remember it for a long time.

Bonding and bridging:

How many of us as children used parts from old bikes, lawn mowers and other equipment to cobble together a go-kart or spaceships or robots? The Swetsville Zoo is the same concept gone wild and a place where you and yours grandchildren can "ooh" and "aah" and ogle each "monster." You can point out the various components of each sculpture and ask them if they can identify others. Better yet, when they come to visit you next time, have a box full of scraps and doodads and some glue, and sit down for a session building your own recycled sculptures—egg cartons, milk cartons, aluminum cans, plastic bottles . . . the options are endless in our throw away society. This is a good opportunity to talk about how we can recycle and reuse more of the things we purchase for our home and meals.

Grandparents will remember the old erector sets where we took plain little pieces of flat metal filled with holes and cobbled together Ferris wheels, trucks and bridges. The other options were Tinker Toys and now, Legos. If you are inspired, pick up some new version and do some creating with your grandchildren. They will enjoy it and you will revel in memories.

A word to the wise:

To some kids, this sculpture garden will look like a playground, but forewarn them that these are not playthings to be climbed upon. As strange as they may seem, these are pieces of art and should be treated with respect as we enjoy them. Needless to say, the possibility of injury on these rusty pieces of metal is not to be taken lightly either. Any rusty metal or parts can cause cuts and those would require tetanus shots. Respect pays dividends.

Age of grandchild: toddler to teenager

Best season: Summer

Contact: 4801 East Harmony Road, Fort Collins, CO 80528

Also check out:

Benson Sculpture Park, Loveland: www.ci.loveland.co.us/parksrec/Benson.htm

Leanin' Tree Museum of Western Art outdoor sculpture garden: www.leanintreemuseum.com/SculptureGarden.asp

Museum of Outdoor Art, Englewood: www.moaonline.org

Rocky Mountain National Park

If you were to ask people to describe their personal image of Colorado, it probably is not the high prairie, the mesa studded west, or even the span of urban development along the front range—it would be the high country, the landscape best captured in the magnificent Rocky Mountain National Park. It is a combination of peaks, valleys, forest, tundra, lakes, and streams so beautiful and so pristine that the Park can represent both Colorado and

the vast sweep of Rocky Mountains that traverse the continent from the Arctic Tundra to the tropics of southern Mexico. Ranging from 8,000 feet to 14,259 feet, you just need to be selective and match your grandchildren to the terrain, the physical challenge and the scenery.

This is where your grandchildren can catch mountain fever, that strong bond with sky high mountains that never leaves many people. Visit the high alpine tundra with its strange rock circles and plants that grow barely an inch tall before the bloom of beautiful and alluring flowers. The willow ptarmigan roams here, a bird as fun and strange as the spelling of its name. A visit to the high country is equal to traveling north to the Arctic Circle. Altitude equals latitude! Talk about giving your grandchildren a trip—let them get their minds around that concept.

Watching for wildlife is a delight to everyone and the Park offers a terrific range of animals that includes elk, mule deer, moose, bighorn sheep, black bears, coyotes, cougars, eagles, hawks, marmots, beaver, ground squirrels, eagles, hawks, osprey, grey and Steller's jays, Clark's nutcrackers and numerous smaller, but very enjoyable birds. Both bird and mammal watchers are rewarded for their efforts in this Park and it is easy to get directions in the Visitor Center for the places where you can optimize your experience.

For your first experience we would recommend Sprague Lake, Bear Lake, or Lily Lake trails. The lake is a focal point for the walk with high mountain vistas in every direction. Waterfowl are often on the waters and you will find good birds along the shore, with an occasional elk and small mammals. Our grandsons love to throw things in the water, so if you or they get tired, a lake gives you a good opportunity to rest and play.

Bonding and bridging:

When I think of my grandparents I often think of them in association with a place. I will always remember them taking me to the Badlands 50 years ago. I remember my grandmother in the blackberry patch. Places and people combine to make magnificent memories. When I travel to Baraboo, Wisconsin I think of my dad. When I am in Steamboat, I think of my great friends Mick and Nancy. We remember our children on certain beaches, our spouses at a cabin or on a sailboat, or some wonderful location where we shared so much. A place like Rocky Mountain National Park has vistas that will always be part of our visual memory. That is why we take photographs and place our loved ones in front of the scenery. It is not because we want to block the natural beauty, but rather because we want to see them amid that beauty. Record your memories in the back of this book.

A word to the wise:

When I open the Rocky Mountain Park newsletter I am pleased with the information I find. There are junior naturalist programs, interpretive hikes, descriptions of trails, and ideas for the visit, but there are also warnings about lightning in the high country, the effect of high altitude, swift waters, high cliffs, wildlife, and avalanches. Read the warnings and take them seriously. They are meant to keep you safe, not keep you out. If you are prepared, you lessen the risks that are in the Park, but at the same time, this is a natural area, a place without handrails and artificial restraints. Common sense protects both us and the Park. Read the warnings and learn.

Age of grandchild: All

Best season: Summer

Contact: 1000 Highway 36, Estes Park, CO 80517-8397 • 970-586-1206
• http://rockymountainnationalpark.com

Also check out:

Black Canyon of the Gunnison National Monument, Montrose: www.nps.gov/blca

Colorado National Monument: www.nps.gov/colm

Florissant Fossil Bed National Monument: www.nps.gov/flfo

Great Sand Dunes National Park: www.nps.gov/grsa

Mesa Verde National Park: www.nps.gov/meve

Some family trees bear an enormous crop of nuts. Wayne H.

Boulder Parks, Greenways, and Green Living

We think that nature and cities are separate places, that we have to leave our community to find trails, trees and birds, but good cities plan greenways and natural settings to provide their citizens with a place to relax, get exercise and keep in touch with the planet's diversity.

Boulder Creek Path, in Boulder, CO, is an easy trail with up to six miles of options and very little elevation change. People jog, bike, stroll and push strollers on this trail and if you want to hike only one way with a shuttle, the trail has a slight incline, so you can walk downhill all the way. The creek adds to the atmosphere and the trail surface is a mix of paved and packed dirt with both sunny and shady sections.

As you decide which green space to enjoy, check the elevation changes. For example, Sawhill ponds, Flatirons Vista, Foothills, Wonderland Lake and Marshall Mesa trails are all easy and you can hike with any age child,

but South Mesa and Chautauqua Royal Arch are more difficult and may not be the right choice for some grandparents and very young grandchildren.

Other parks are scattered throughout the community, which takes great pride in being green. Boulder limits population growth, as well as the height of buildings, to make sure that the surrounding scenery is shared by everyone. They have a green building code and emphasize recycling. They encourage bicyclists, and a sense of health and vigor among the citizens is apparent. The parks are also the sites for community celebrations and events like EcoArts, a gathering of scientists and artists to talk about climate change. This celebrates a sustainable future and includes art exhibitions, science activities for kids and adults, and exhibits and demonstrations about sustainable living. And EcoArts is unique because of the range of experiences, including dance, performance and even a Wind Parade.

These type of experiences emphasize that play is a form of learning, celebration is a way of uniting our spirit for good, and nature is our source of renewal. The parks are yours, use them and enjoy them.

Bonding and bridging:

This community allows you to explore how people and nature can co-exist, how we can take care of the earth and still enjoy quality of life. Boulder has been included in a variety of "best of" lists like "the Best Outside Towns," "The Top Five Cities for Cycling," and the "Top Town for Triathlons." In 2007, there were 70 Olympians living in the community. The annual Bolder Boulder was the second largest 10K road race in the country, with over 51,000 participants, many of whom did not care about winning, but wanted to be part of the event, even if they walked.

This city provides lessons for visitors to take home and challenges many of our perceptions about pollution and urban blight. It provides lessons for visitors to take home to their communities and their own property. Can we live a lifestyle that will provide for a healthy future? Is there a connection between people who care for the earth and community and those who care for their own health and bodies?

A word to the wise:

Parks are truly ethical parts of urban design, and they represent a variety of things to different people. Bird watchers do not go to the same places as softball players, and bikers and joggers do not seek swings and slides, but all these locations are parks. Parks make statements about who we are and what we believe is valuable. When we say "park" to our grandchildren they think swings, slides, and playgrounds. Be aware if you simply use the term "park," you and your grandchildren might have different expectations. Instead, be specific. Say, "let's go for a walk, let's go bird watching, let's go fishing, let's play ball"—then you all will be pleased when you get to your destination.

Age of grandchild: All

Best season: All

Contact: City of Boulder, 1777 Broadway, Boulder, CO 80302 • (303) 441-3410 • www.ci.boulder.co.us

Also check out:

Fort Collins Parks: www.ci.fort-collins.co.us

www.ecoartsonline.org

www.GoBikeBoulder.net

Life is no brief candle to me. It is a sort of splendid torch which I've got hold of for the moment and I want to make it burn as brightly as possible before handing it on to the future generations. George Bernard Shaw

National Center for Atmospheric Research

You probably read this name and thought—what kind of place is this to take my grandchildren? Well, think again. Perched half way up the Front Range, high meadows of mountain flowers roll from the dramatic laboratory building into the peaks, and trails invite you to stroll through the open landscape, but stop! That massive building, designed to look like the ancient Mesa Verde

cliff dwellings (the architect really had an imagination) is startling in its placement with the natural landscape, but it is also perfect for giving your grandchildren a real dose of science. It might not be a yellow brick road from the parking lot, but the statues and the walkway still feel a little like a journey to Oz.

There is nothing more basic to our lives than weather, or the accumulation of weather over time which is climate. To understand either requires science and this amazing facility is all about science and inquiry. From the Computer room in the basement, your journey upward takes you to the weather exhibits in the lobby and on the mezzanine, and finally to climate and the sun on the second floor.

There are three-dimensional experiences with lots of hands-on discovery that will tempt the grandparents and grandchildren to become involved. Attend the theater and see the movies and enjoy the art galleries, as these experiences include science.

Learning about our atmosphere, our sun, and our earth has been the challenge for generations. From balloons to rockets, we have set out to explore and to understand, but it is a big challenge with big concepts to understand.

Go outdoors and walk the Walter Orr Roberts weather trail; the trail does not include a variety of weather, but it does include a variety of stories set in whatever the weather of your visit might be. You can watch for clouds forming as air moves over the mountains, you can see the paths fire left, note the differences in moisture and feel the impact of wind. The exercise is good for both mind and body.

Bonding and bridging:

We all listen to the weather forecasts and often change our plans because of them; yet weather is such a mystery to us and climate is so complex that we can understand it only by keeping long-term records, not by the conditions of a given day or week. So think about making weather a part of your life in another way. The Center's store has great weather equipment and guides.

Use this adventure to help your grandchild start a lifetime of observation. Encourage them to record the temperature, measure the rainfall, and record wind direction and speed. You can do the same. Identify the cloud types and how the wind direction changes during the day. But do not use just electronic gauges, actually measure them. The physical activity is important. If your grandchildren live in another city or even another state or country they can still do this and you can share and compare. Compare your readings with the local forecaster and keep track of their predictions and their accuracy.

A word to the wise:

The impact of weather and climate is part of every day's decisions, including at home and at the office. Heating and cooling are a response to the sun, and our roofs provide both shade and shelter from the rain. We have used a lot of different strategies for our survival, but today we realize that learning about the elements of weather—wind, sun, shade, and moisture—can actually allow us to control our environment without destroying it. We call these options renewable energy and the National Renewable Energy Laboratory in Golden has a Visitor Center with displays and information that is a perfect follow-up to your discoveries about weather and climate.

Age of grandchild: 10 and up

Contact: Visitor Center, 1850 Table Mesa Drive, Boulder, CO 80305 • (303) 497-1174 • http://eo.ucar.edu/visit

Also check out:

Colorado Climate Center (web access only): http://ccc.atmos.colostate.edu

National Renewable Energy Laboratory, NREL visitor center, 15013 Denver West Parkway, Golden, CO 80401-3393; (303) 384-6565; www.nrel.gov

Butterfly Pavilion and Insect Center

Insects are the outcasts of the animal world, right up there with reptiles in many people's minds. "Cute" and "cuddly" they aren't, yet they make up the largest group of living beings in the animal kingdom. And we absolutely need them. If all the insects, or even very important ones like bees, disappeared tomorrow—we humans would soon follow.

As naturalists, we are fascinated with insects and we're trying to transfer that fascination to our grandchildren. The Butterfly Pavilion and Insect Center is a great place to foster that interest.

The Crawl-A-See-Em is filled with display cases containing all manner of "creepy crawlies"—the kind that might cause you to wrinkle your nose or draw back, but make an effort to restrain your initial reactions, so that the grandkids can see them as they are—strange, but amazing, animals. One of these displays is the "Tarantula Tower" and it contains 16 different species of this spider, but most exciting is Rosie, the tarantula. A volunteer Docent will be sitting with Rosie in one corner and if your grandchildren or you wish, they can let her rest in the palm of their hand. If they do, they get a special sticker to wear.

Another room called the Water's Edge has a touch tank with sea stars and sea urchins that the kids can touch. Another tank has lobsters swimming in it and there is a TV playing videos of underwater life.

The main room, the Tropical Conservatory, is a lush garden, with over 1,200 butterflies of all hues and sizes flitting through the moist air. A stream flows through the room, adding a soothing sound. There is a magical feeling in a room like this. The only rule is to not touch the butterflies, even if they land nearby. Butterflies are released into the room twice a day, at scheduled times. A display case holds a number of chrysalides; check it periodically if you want to see one emerge.

Near the end of your visit, stop by the Shrunk! room, where the kids can climb and scramble over and through a giant honeycomb and up a rope "web." Other giant insects are animated—ants come out of a nest, a praying mantis moves its head, and a scorpion raises its tail.

Bonding and bridging:

Finding butterfly chrysalides in the wild is almost impossible, but raising caterpillars is an educational project you and your grandchildren can do together. In Colorado this would happen in the early summer, once the monarchs return to the area and begin to lay eggs on milkweed plants. A short time later, you can hunt for caterpillars and bring them home on their host plant—put them in a big jar or a special box, with screen sides and watch as it changes in size and finally shapes a protective green chrysalis. 12-14 days later it emerges as a beautiful black and orange butterfly. Let your grandchildren name the butterfly as you release it into the air.

Monarchs spend the winter months in the mountains of Central Mexico. They live tenuous lives, threatened by deforestation in Mexico and loss of milkweeds here in the U.S.; many people consider milkweed a pest and try to get rid of them with herbicides. By raising a few monarch butterflies, we are doing a little to help the species, and we are showing our grandchildren that we care, even for insects.

A word to the wise:

Outside of the Pavilion there are gardens and a trail which give you and your grandchild a chance to look for "wild" butterflies, landing on flowers that have been planted especially for them. The garden is "xeriscaped," designed to demonstrate the best plantings for Colorado's dry and sunny conditions. A trail meanders down toward a stand of cottonwoods and a stream, so be prepared for a few minutes of pebble tossing. Look for prairie dogs and rabbits on either side of the trail. The prairie dogs in particular are a treat as they pop up and squeak in alarm, then disappear down into their dens.

Age of grandchild: 2 to 10

Contact: 6252 West 104th Ave., Westminster, CO 80020
• (303)-469-5441 • www.butterflies.org

Also check out:

Denver Botanical Garden: www.botanicgardens.org

Denver Zoo, Denver: www.denverzoo.org

Pueblo Zoo, Pueblo: www.pueblozoo.org

Western Colorado Botanical Gardens and Butterfly House, Grand Junction: www.wcbotanic.org

Georgetown Loop
and Lebanon Gold Mine

Railroads and mines keep coming up as you travel Colorado or look at the options for travel, tourism, learning, and engaging. These are the remnants of Colorado's historic pioneer past and helped settlers climb the mountain passes, where they pitched their tents, and dug in the rock. There, they built bridges, laid track, and dreamed of the iron horse.

Mines and railroads come together at the Georgetown Loop where an historic engine pulls you and many others into the past and lets you see the past era without the problems, dangers, and uncertainty that faced the early Coloradoans. Because it is a loop, you can catch the train from either Georgetown (actually not right in the town) or Silver Plume. We would recommend Silver Plume and you should spend some time walking around in the small town before or after the ride. The town is still alive and doing well, but remnants of its mining past give it the feeling of a ghost town as well. The town is up against the mountain and many buildings and structures date to the days of the Pelican Mine.

The train depot is just across the freeway from Silver Plume and is a fun structure that puts you in the right frame of mind. A red depot with a wooden walkway, this feels like an authentic starting point for an old west railroad and the whistle and steam from the locomotive will signal the next stage in your exploration. This loop railroad connected two towns just two miles apart in 1884 on a route that was called a "corkscrew." Today it takes you over a tall bridge (Devil's Gate) and past beautiful rapids, on a 4% grade.

From 1899 to 1938 it served as a part of the Colorado and Southern Railway. In 1973 the old line was restored as part of a 978 acre Historic Mining and Railroad park. You can include the historic Lebanon Silver Mine as part of the experience. Ride the loop, get off at the mine and rejoin the train afterward—you do not lose any part of the ride. The Mine is part of the Hise Lode, 1,100 feet below the entrance with veins that are rich with silver. The tunnel is 1,200 feet long, but silver prices, not a lack of silver, stopped the operation. Now the mine is yours to experience and the combination is memorable.

Bonding and bridging:

Why do we dig holes? What compels us to search for treasure? Pirates' buried treasures are part of our cultural history; today's treasures are easily imagined riches, like lotteries and casinos. In some ways searching for treasure is a form of hide and seek; in other ways it is a sign of greed and avarice.

We seek underwater treasures, we have scavenger hunts and we engage in lots of activities that we hope will lead to a prize, a reward, or a treasure. Why? It is worth talking to your grandchildren about this. Why is gold and silver more valuable in a vault than in the ground? Why does one metal have a higher value than another? What makes jewelry valuable? What is the difference between values and valuables?

A word to the wise:

The mine is cold, like all underground places, and you need to prepare. It is also dark; be ready for this darkness. Even though the path is lighted, there are dark recesses and too often we scare our children with monsters and scary things lurking in the dark places. Give them a warm jacket, let them carry a flashlight and let them enjoy the dark. The dark should not be an enemy.

Age of grandchild: 3 to 12

Best season: Summer

Contact: Georgetown Loop Railroad, P.O. Box 249, Georgetown, CO 80444 • (888) 456-6777 • www.georgetownlooprr.com

Also check out:

Bacelor-Syracuse Mine tour, Ouray: www.bachelorsyracusemine.com

Durango-Silverton Railroad, Durango and Silverton: www.durangotrain.com

Georgetown: http://town.georgetown.co.us

Leadville, Colorado and Southern Railroad, Leadville: www.leadville-train.com

National Mining Hall of Fame, Leadville: www.mininghalloffame.org

Rio Grande Scenic Railroad: www.riograndescenicrailroad.com

Royal Gorge Railroad, Canon City: www.royalgorgeroute.com

Silver Plume: www.townofsilverplume.org/townsite/Home.html

I don't intentionally spoil my grandkids. It's just that correcting them often takes more energy than I have left. GENE PERRET

31

Dinosaur Ridge Visitor Center

A tracker will tell you that we leave many clues with every step we take. Our tracks tell how big we are, how many legs we have and details like whether we step harder with one foot than the other, lean to one side, and our direction of travel. Well, imagine this—dinosaurs walked here! It was a very long time ago, but like us they left their footprints and we can learn a lot by studying them. Dinosaur Ridge is one of the classic places to see ancient tracks, tracks so old that the mud and the sand they were made in has turned to stone.

There is a road that takes us through the layers of rock—much of it tilted up instead of lying flat like it did during dinosaur times. This means that the Rocky Mountains are newer than the tracks. Now that is old.

Dinosaur Ridge has a Visitor Center to help you understand what you see and it includes some dramatic fossils like a huge spine in the rock next to the driveway—see if you can find this and other artifacts from dinosaur days. Maybe you can measure and draw these fossils to record your knowledge for later reference. The road has many places to explore with the highlight being the footprint rocks. Follow the signs; touch the rocks where it is allowed.

Time is the hardest thing for us to understand. We know an hour, a day and even a lifetime, but we don't understand a million years. To help, there is a time-line for you to walk. This means translating distance into large chunks of time, something even an adult has a hard time understanding, but you can understand that some events are closer together or closer to the present than others. This simple exercise of "closer" and "farther" does give some perspective on history, a history that took place long before humans filled the earth.

Colorado is filled with places to explore the dinosaur era and each place like this will help make the reconstructed dinosaurs in the museums and videos much more real.

Bonding and bridging:

Make this an adventure in tracking. Show your grand-children the tracks they make. Look at tire tracks, footprints, and other signs that might be around you. Even litter is a track that tells a story about the person who left it. Then use this exploration as the beginning of an adventure that can take you all around the state. The next stop should be near Boulder at the Triceratops Trail. Show them a picture. Try to figure out the animal's size and then set off to observe, take pictures and investigate.

This path is right next to a golf course. Imagine if they could come back and walk across the greens! In one half mile you will go back 68 million years, traveling through an ancient swamp. There might be insects, bones, teeth, and claws, as well as tracks. But in reality, what you find is not as important as the realization that you are walking in the path of an ancient giant.

A word to the wise:

While the fossils, museums, and explorations are wonderful, you can't take them home like books and posters. But perhaps the best way to build on what you see is by DVD with the series "Walking with Dinosaurs. The BBC worked with paleontologists to develop the most realistic film reconstruction of dinosaurs that you could ever watch. It shows the animals in interactions between species and the plants and landscapes that they shared. It is a wonderful film experience and has special features that show actual digs and background details.

Age of grandchild: 5 to 12

Best season: Summer

Contact: Dinosaur Ridge Visitor Center, 16831 W. Alameda Pkwy, Morrison, CO 80465 • (303) 697-3466 • www.dinoridge.org

Also check out:

Dinosaur Diamond National Scenic Byway: www.dinosaurdiamond.org

Dinosaur Journey/Museum of Western Colorado: www.dinosaurjourney.org

Dinosaur Resource Center, Woodland Park: www.rmdrc.com

Dinosaur Trails of Fruita: www.co.blm.gov/mcnca/index.htm

Picketwire Canyon: www.sangres.com/nationalparks/dinosaur

Through my grandmother's eyes, I can see more clearly the way things used to be, the way things ought to be, and most important of all, the way things really are. Ed Cunningham

Colorado Railroad Museum

In the state with the biggest variety of railroad rides, it seems redundant to go to a location where the railroad cars and engines simply sit on their tracks, but the trains that you ride do not offer the same opportunity to explore, climb, and learn that this magnificent collection provides. While it is fun to sit and watch the countryside go by, there is something special about climbing up into an engine, walking beside the huge cars, or exploring a caboose.

This is the largest railroad museum in the Rocky Mountain West and the variety of cars and lines represented here give you some idea of the age of rails responsible for tying the east and west together. Spread over 14 acres, numerous railroad cars are open for your inspection, while the roundhouse holds others being restored for future years. While your grandchildren may not find this exciting, you might enjoy the fact that even the rails are historic with some dating back to 1882.

You enter through the gift store, but put that off until the end. Downstairs is a model train set that will entice your grandchildren to observe and enjoy, it will be familiar for them, like Thomas the Tank Engine. This will help bridge the gap between toy trains and the real railroad cars outside.

You will all enjoy the variety of engines and railroad cars, including the original cog wheel train that went up Pike's Peak. If you choose to ride up to Pike's Peak during your explorations, this train will have extra meaning. Then there are the Galloping Geese! These strange trains were actually built from cars (Buicks and Pierce Arrows) to haul both passengers and mail between Durango, Telluride, and Ridgway in the southwest mountains.

But trains are not just engines—there are passenger cars, mail cars, freight cars, and cabooses. Each is a different design, limited by the width of the tracks and the power of the engine. Explore each one, climb in and get the feeling of being on the tracks. This is living history and each car has a place and a story.

Bonding and bridging:

Railroads had a real impact on communities. Today the freeway, the airport or the size of the port determine the success and growth of a community. Transportation is part of America and you can share the story of how we move and move our goods so your grandchildren understand both the importance and the problems of transportation.

As grandchildren get older you can talk about our mobile world and business, but perhaps you can start by talking about why Europe still uses so many railroads and we do not. Would it be better if we had more rails in our cities and between cities? Why did we move away from railroads? Why are we in a hurry? When we travel, we affect the world around us. What are our options and our responsibilities?

A word to the wise:

The Denver Garden Railway Society and the Denver model railroad (H.O. club) work together to create a landscaped model train experience. This train does not run everyday, so call to check schedules. This miniature railroad set is the next step up from the model trains and can easily capture your grandchildren's imagination. The larger scale makes the trains seem quite real, especially with the landscaping done so well. For young children, the Thomas the Tank Engine experiences can be impressive and memorable. There is also a Santa Claus Express and a Bunny Express and the School's Out train. If you are bothered by many children running around, choose to come another day.

Age of grandchild: 3 to 12

Best season: Summer

Contact: 17155 West 44th Avenue, Golden, CO 80403 • (800) 365-6263 • www.crrm.org

Also Check Out:

Durango-Silverton Railroad Durango: www.durangotrain.com

Georgetown Loop Railroad: http://georgetownlooprr.com

Leadville, Colorado and Southern Railroad: www.leadville-train.com

Rio Grande Scenic Railroad: www.riograndescenicrailroad.com

Royal Gorge Railroad: www.royalgorgeroute.com

Tiny Town

People have been drawn to this Lilliputian town since the days when the only way to get here was up a narrow and winding dirt road. Thankfully, the trip is much quicker and safer today as you travel up Hwy 285, but the charm and fun are just as real as when George Turner built the village (called Turnerville) for his daughter in 1915. The town is a child's fantasy, where the buildings are 1/6 scale. Turner would be pleased to see that the village is still entertaining children and adults alike, nearly 100 years after he built it.

The fact that it does still exist is a tribute to the persistence and dreams of many people, because it has opened and closed no fewer than three times and was nearly demolished by floods and fire. In 1989, a non-profit foundation was formed to make sure that it will continue to be a successful attraction for future generations of children.

Although it wasn't part of the original layout, a miniature (15 inch gauge) train is part of the village; its steam locomotive pulls passengers around the outskirts of the village, along Turkey Creek, and past a hillside with its own collection of miniature buildings. It's a toss up which is more fun for the kids—peering into these oversized dollhouses or riding the train. There are more than 100 buildings on the site. Many are replicas of the original structures that Turner built, although the original village had roadways and fountains and even an adult-sized Pueblo. Many of the current buildings are replicas of famous Colorado landmarks, such as Denver's original Fire Station and the Coney Island Hot Dog stand. The buildings are small enough that toddlers can stand and look in the windows, while adults have to bend or squat down to see inside. Some have dolls and furniture appropriate to the structure. Others are open in the back, so that the kids can go inside.

Even though Tiny Town sits in a mountain canyon, between the towns of Morrison and Conifer, the paved path that loops around the village is level and easy to navigate on foot or pushing a stroller. There is a nice, shaded picnic area, with a playground close by, so you can pack a picnic for your visit.

Bonding and bridging:

Since this venue is really geared to the younger grand-children, it isn't likely that you will engage them in discussions of the history of the place or even your history. This is a place to suspend your normal adult perspective of the world and try to see it again through the eyes of the children; to experience wonder and delight by a world turned upside down. Express surprise and delight with the grandchildren as you move from building to building. Their enjoyment will increase because of yours. In your own home consider building or buying a small dollhouse or farm, or other structure where you and the grandkids can engage in make believe play. Or get out some paper and have them sit down and design the town of the future, the one they'd like to live in.

If you can find a nice illustrated *Gulliver's Travels* by Jonathan Swift they might enjoy comparing the Lilliputian village to this one and see how the adults must feel in a town that is just right for them.

A word to the wise:

On busy summer weekends, the line for the train ride can be long and hot. Little ones generally have little patience when told to stand in line. Bring beverages and snacks to help ease the wait and maybe a toy or two. It also helps if one grandparent can hold the place in line, so the children do not have to stand still in the sun. The Tiny Town gift store is also located right next to the train boarding spot, so be prepared for kids drawn by the toys and other items there.

Age of grandchild: toddler to 8 years

Best season: Summer

Contact: 6249 S. Turkey Creek Rd, Morrison, CO 80465
• (303) 697-6829 • www.tinytownrailroad.com

Also check out:

Denver Doll Emporium: www.denverdoll.com

Denver Museum of Miniatures, Dolls, and Toys: www.dmmdt.org

It's funny what happens when you become a grandparent. You start to act all goofy and do things you never thought you'd do. It's terrific. MIKE KRZYZEWSKI

Hammond's Candy Factory

Who doesn't love candy? Most of us never outgrow the "sweet tooth" we had as kids. Grandparents have always been the purveyors of sweets for the grandkids, sometimes to the chagrin of their parents, but we know it isn't going to cause permanent damage, and in fact, will probably create permanent memories of special moments with grandma or grandpa. Mike still talks about the special box of chocolates his grandfather kept in his desk drawer and how he'd offer Mike one per day. We grandparents all have memories of certain

candies that were our favorite. Mine were the penny candies—root beer barrels, Lik'm Aid, and red licorice strings, or the cherry cordials that my grandmother had at her house on special occasions. Where have all those great candies gone? Sure, some of the same candy bars are around—although they've been supersized, but most have disappeared.

It's still possible to find candy reminiscent of our youth. Hammond's Candy Factory has been in existence since the 1920s. Today it is in a nondescript industrial warehouse strip, with bright red lettering above the windows. Walk through the doors and you are immediately greeted by that captivating sugar smell—like cotton candy being spun. Three year old grandson Aren, a born sugar fanatic, knew immediately he was in a very special place. "Candy," he announced, his eyes lighting up. The entry area has soda parlor style tables and some glass display cases with memorabilia from the early years of the company. Since you often have to wait for the next tour, the company has wisely placed crayons and coloring paper out for the entertainment of impatient little ones. There are also some free samples to help get them started.

With the kids wearing paper hats just like the ones soda jerks used to wear, you go to a room to watch an "educational" (promotional really) video about the making of the sweets. Then you move to a hallway where you can see the workers wearing special gloves, pulling, stretching, cutting and shaping lollipops, candy canes and more. You proceed down the hallway, watching the lumps elongate and get cut as they move through a variety of machines. At the end of the line, there are more machines creating chocolate bunnies and other treats. Finally, your tour guide lets you pick out a piece of wrapped candy from a giant bucket. Then you are escorted into the sales room where candy lines the walls and fills the display cases.

Bonding and bridging:

Obviously, this is a commercial enterprise, but there is enough of a connection to the candies of our time to give you opportunities to talk about how you felt about candy as a child, when you got it and why. Having a special candy dish or drawer in your own home and making it a special treat, at a special time of day, when they visit is another way to create an indelible memory of time spent with you. Watching Willy Wonka and the Chocolate Factory together might be a fun follow up to the Candy Factory.

We have found it fun to order old classic candies from The Old Time Candy Company. Check out their website at: www.oldtimecandy.com. How do you think candy was developed? What was the first candy? Some say it was started with cavemen drying out honey into a taffy-like consistency. But for commercial candy we have to look to 1854 when Whitman produced the first boxed candy which was much better than gum made from spruce sap! Valentine boxes started in 1858. Look how candy has become a symbol— and is found in Easter baskets, Valentine hearts and Christmas Candy Canes.

A word to the wise:

Be sure to set some limits before going to the Candy Factory—either how much money they can spend on candy or how many pieces they can buy. The last thing you want to experience is a temper tantrum. Check with the parents too, to make sure they are OK with the visit and if there are any particular rules about how much candy the kids can have and when they can have it. It might be a good idea to have the grandkids pick out one or two treats for their parents. How can they object when they get to enjoy part of the visit too?

Age of grandchild: 3 to 12

Best season: Any

Contact: 5735 N Washington Street, Denver, CO 80216 • (303) 333-5588
• www.hammondscandies.com

Also check out:

Mountain Man Fruits and Nuts, Highland Ranch: www.mountainmanhighlandsranch.com

Story of Jolly Ranchers, Golden Pioneer Museum: www.goldenpioneermuseum.com/documents/jollyrancher_ae.htm

Family faces are magic mirrors. Looking at people who belong to us, we see the past, present and future. GAIL LUMET BUCKLEY

Children's Museum of Denver

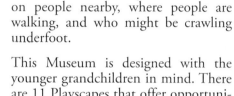

Is this a museum or a playground? Does it matter? To the kids there is no question about what the museum is—it is their place. Even the exterior has the look of colorful building blocks. Color, design, and educational content are interwoven into one of the most child-engaging places possible. It is the job of the grandparent to guide them through, letting the children's imagination make the choices, while you watch over safety and the possible conflict that can arise from lots of little hands and feet concentrating on fun and not on people nearby, where people are walking, and who might be crawling underfoot.

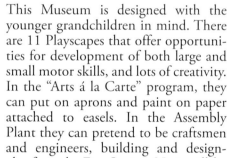

This Museum is designed with the younger grandchildren in mind. There are 11 Playscapes that offer opportunities for development of both large and small motor skills, and lots of creativity. In the "Arts á la Carte" program, they can put on aprons and paint on paper attached to easels. In the Assembly Plant they can pretend to be craftsmen and engineers, building and designing objects with recycled materials and safe tools. Fire Station No.1 will be a magnet, since it's a real fire engine that they can climb aboard and act out the role of the firefighter. In addition, there is an interactive 911 call center, where you can practice the steps to follow in a real emergency. It's amazing what little minds can remember after even one practice session.

This is creative play, and imagination is the real tool that will lead to creative thinking, problem solving, and intuitive response in later life. Sometimes it is necessary to cajole and make sure that there is sharing, but don't turn into a bully even on behalf of your grandchildren. Let the children learn how to play together, as well as fantasize in the world constructed by each display.

Think about the way children try to emulate adults. Here they are encouraged to act out the roles they have created in their minds. They are offered adult settings but not told how to fulfill the roles they choose. Whether it takes place on a fire engine, a market, or a basketball court—the story is theirs to create.

The Museum sees the role of grandparents as essential to the children and offers a membership at less than the Family rate. It is a very good deal!

Bonding and bridging:

In play, the children look for approval, and grandparents are ideal candidates to encourage, praise, and offer new insights. It is an important role and the grandparents need to allow the child to have the experience—that means stepping back and letting the children explore. Let your grandchildren experiment with different methods of problem-solving. Keep your suggestions to a minimum, and offer guidance only as a last resort. When they have completed the activity, challenge them by asking ""How did that work?" "What did you like best and why?" You will be sending your grandchildren a message that there isn't always just one answer, and it's okay to make mistakes, as long as you learn from them. Help them learn to pace themselves (a very tough task) and process the things they learn.

A word to the wise:

This is your day to enable and observe. Take advantage of the Museum's Story time, held each day at 11:20 (weekdays) and noon (weekends). The Museum staff chooses a theme for each story time and includes crafts afterward. And when it feels overwhelming, let the children know that Grandpa or Grandma is a little tired and if they will go to one of the quiet areas with you and relax with you a while, they can stay even longer. Story time is the time to hook kids on books. Make sure you continue it at home and maybe pick up one of the books they experienced at the museum.

Age of grandchild: infant to 8

Best season: All

Contact: 2121 Children's Museum Drive, Denver, CO 80211
• (303) 433-7444 • www.cmdenver.org

Also check out:

Check websites since museums vary with their special programs and hours

Buell Children's Museum, Pueblo: www.sdc-arts.org/bcc.html

Mountain Top Children's Museum, Breckenridge: www.mtntopmuseum.org

The Children's Museum of Durango, Durango: www.childsmuseum.org

WOW Children's Museum, Lafayette: www.wowmuseum.com

Teaching children about the natural world should be treated as one of the most important events in their lives. THOMAS BERRY, DREAM OF THE EARTH

Downtown Aquarium

In 2003 the Ocean Journey Aquarium—a publicly funded educational institution—was purchased by the Landry Restaurant chain. It was subsequently remodeled and revamped to accommodate dining opportunities. The exhibits, which cover 14 ecosystems, remain, and many of the graphics contain good information, but most of the interactive components of the earlier Aquarium are gone.

The fish and various other sea life are still the stars and all ages of kids will enjoy the colorful and sometimes bizarre looking denizens of the deep. A combination of live mammals (including Sumatran tigers) and animatrons

are scattered about, including an animatronic orangutan and her baby sitting on rocks in the misty rainforest exhibit. Some of these artificial animals may cause some confusion for the younger grandkids.

The Desert exhibit has an adrenaline raising fake flash flood that older grandkids will thoroughly enjoy and they may even learn something about the dynamics of hydrology in desert canyons. As you walk through the exhibits you may also see divers in the water. Some may even be up against the glass cleaning it from the inside. Artificial rocks and plants cover the walls of the aquarium as you move from one region to the next. Some tanks are small and located on the walls, while many are large with floor-to-ceiling glass for wide angle viewing. In the Shipwreck exhibit, you can stand on round glass portholes and look down upon sleeping sharks. There is much to amaze and entertain the children in the Aquarium and it will be largely up to you, the grandparent, to add the educational component.

Aquariums are a passive way to explore the world of fish and especially the life of the ocean. It is like snorkeling without having to put on a mask and fins. The life forms are alien, which makes them intriguing. They are also colorful and mesmerizing in their free-floating patterns. If your grandchildren are interested and old enough, you can arrange for them to be marine biologists or zoologists for a day and you might also consider an aquarium for home.

Bonding and bridging:

Since this is really a dining/entertainment complex, you may want to include a meal as a special part of your visit, depending on the age of the grandchildren. Glass walls allow you to watch the fish slowly pass by as you wait for your meal to arrive. It will also allow you to talk about our oceans and how important they are to all of us. This will be especially true if you have ordered fish of some sort. Denver is in the middle of the North American continent, but children need to know that tuna and fish sticks come from the sea, that fish are a food resource, just like livestock grown on farms. We must manage them carefully, and not overharvest such resources if we hope to have them around for the future. Older grandkids may already be aware of the restrictions on certain types of seafood because of mercury contamination. They may even be able to tell you why this is happening.

A word to the wise:

If your grandchildren have ever traveled to tropical waters, or dream of doing so, you can arrange a special snorkel adventure in the large tank where you and they can swim with the flashy angel fish and humongous Queensland grouper. Children must be 6 years and older to participate and there is a fee, of course. Also be aware that weekday trips during the month of May will be especially crowded, since this is the peak time for school field trips. You may be overwhelmed with hundreds of excited, elementary students, who crowd around and make it difficult to get next to the stingray pool, where visitors have a chance to feed and touch these exotic and ancient creatures of the deep. Younger grandchildren may be intimidated and hesitant to touch the stingrays. You can always hold your grandchildren or let them stand next to the pool and watch others.

Age of grandchild: 3 to 14

Best season: Any

Contact: 700 Water St., Denver, CO 80211 • (303) 561-4450 • www.aquariumrestaurants.com/downtownaquariumdenver/flash_content/index.html

Also check out:

Hotchkiss Fish Hatchery, Delta: www.fws.gov/hotchkiss

Leadville National Fish Hatchery, Leadville: www.fws.gov/leadville/info.htm

Sunshine is delicious, rain is refreshing, wind braces us up, snow is exhilarating; there's really no such thing as bad weather, only different kinds of good weather. JOHN RUSKIN

Black American West Museum

If you are like us, and like many grandparents, you grew up on a diet of cowboy television and movies that had one thing in common—the cowboys were all white guys. There was an occasional Indian, like Tonto, to break up the monotony, but overall Mike's heroes were guys like Hopalong Cassidy, Wyatt Earp, Roy Rogers and on and on. The movies were just as bland—with the white John Wayne and a handful of western stars playing every cowboy and hero of the American West. Through the age of the western we continued to not only disregard the heroism and life of American Indians, we also forgot to tell everyone that one third of those cowpokes were African Americans!

Oh, the lies we learn when we fail to investigate. But no more! There is no reason to be uninformed about the West and the role freed slaves played: The Black American Museum will help set the record straight. It is located in the home of Dr. Justina Ford, the first African American doctor in Denver, on the corner of a residential city block. Because she was a black woman, she could not practice in a hospital at that time, so this home was also her office and clinic—an unimposing site with its own history.

It was not the doctor who dreamed of telling the true story of the western cowboy, but Paul W. Stewart, who began to collect books and artifacts that have now been incorporated into the displays you see. The Museum is small, but the story is not. When you enter and explore Stewart's life and learn about his desire to capture the lost stories of black cowboys, you appreciate the artifacts and stories even more.

They have enough items of pioneer life and the cattle drive to give you some atmosphere for discovering the stories of "Deadwood Dick" A.K.A. Nat Love, Bill Pickett, Inventor of "Bull Dogging," the famous mountain man James Beckwourth and Clara Brown, "Angel of the Rockies."

Black Americans weren't only cowboys; they were also Buffalo Soldiers (a name given to African American soldiers by Native Americans, according to legend), and an African American slave, York, even accompanied Lewis and Clark on their way to the Pacific.

Bonding and bridging:

This museum introduces new stories and new perspectives of Black Americans, but leaves you wanting more. This is a special opportunity for you to participate in research and learning with your grandchildren. Start with the library near you and search their books, their magazines, their archives. Knowledge about the Black American West will result.

Then explore the Internet, a world that might be more comfortable for the grandchildren than many grandparents and look for resources like www.blackcowboys.com/blackcowboys.htm and http://social.chass.ncsu.edu/slatta/essays/blackcowboys.htm. Visit other resources like the Blair-Caldwell African American Research Library and Stiles African American Heritage Center and state and local historical societies.

A word to the wise:

In addition to visiting the Museum and doing some research, it is also good to connect your experiences. Keep in mind what you learned in this Museum as you visit other Old West museums, ghost towns, and historical museums. Make sure you look for people of color in the story of the West and allow your grandchildren to have a better and more accurate view of our country's history. For example, Chinese immigrants laid the foundation for the railroads and were active in trade and commerce in communities as well, but were seldom appreciated for what they contributed. Indians were the original people of the West and some went on to work as cowboys as the West changed. And Mexicans were vaqueros—cowboys who were much more than the Cisco Kid and Ponchos portrayed on televisions. Put all these people together and the West really does come alive.

Age of grandchild: 5 and up

Best season: Summer

Contact: 3091 California St, Denver, CO 80205 • (303) 482-2242 • www.blackamericanwestmuseum.com

Also check out:

Colorado History Museum, Denver: www.colorado.com/Listing.aspx?did=2062

Pro Rodeo Hall of Fame, Colorado Springs: www.prorodeohalloffame.com

Denver Zoo

Eighty acres are dedicated within Denver's historic City Park to the Denver Zoo, which opened its Bear Mountain exhibit in 1918. That exhibit is a National Historic Landmark and still in use, although it was renovated in 1987. It was ahead of its time in terms of creating a natural look with artificial rock work, based on casts of natural rock near Morrison, Colorado. The Zoo has continued over the years to renovate and innovate, and has created larger and more natural exhibits for the animals.

Monkey Island is a real island (built in 1936 as a WPA project) with large cottonwood trees growing in the center, and even though the Capuchin mon-

keys would not find these kinds of trees in their native forests, it is nice to see them climbing among the green, leafy branches. The same can be said for the Primate Panorama where western lowland gorillas roam a one acre exhibit and the orangutans can also access an equally green space.

Zoos are constantly striving to provide their animals with challenging and mentally stimulating activities, to challenge them in ways that are similar to the challenges they would meet if they were in the wild. In that spirit, the Denver Zoo recently added a "shipwreck" to the polar bear exhibit. Each morning before the great bears go out on exhibit, the keepers hide fish and other treats in nooks and crannies of the ship. This not only enriches the bears' day, but it gives the visitor a chance to see the animals engaged in more natural behavior.

Three large, newer buildings contain interesting animals and exhibits. They are the Tropical Discovery, the Emerald Forest, and Bird World. A winter day might be just when you need a trip to a tropical destination and in the Tropical Discovery building you will find a lush setting with waterfalls, jungle scenes and dark, damp caves. This is where the Komodo dragon lives. Just the word "dragon" is sure to bring a sparkle of excitement to your grandchild's eyes.

There is a carousel and a miniature train at this Zoo, but hopefully you and your grandchild will find the nearly 4000 animals to be more than enough entertainment for one day. This is a Zoo that requires a lot of walking, so you might want to limit what you see per visit. Strollers and wagons can be rented to help little ones when their stamina gives out.

Bonding and bridging:

There is a variety of excitement you can only find in a zoo, one shared by young and old alike. We're fascinated by animals, especially those we rarely see. We can watch them from a safe distance and marvel at their grace and beauty.

The zoo also gives us a chance to talk about nature. Why are some animals endangered? What can we do to help them survive? Polar bears are in the news a lot and kids may know that they are threatened by global warming. They empathize with animals, and want to be good caretakers. We grandparents should nurture that empathy. Together you can talk about ways of reducing CO_2 that leads to climate change. Use this time to help your grandchildren appreciate animals and foster a concern for the environment. By doing so we may help save some endangered species for future generations to enjoy, and when we save animal species we also enrich the earth, making it healthier for life and thereby making it healthier for us.

A word to the wise:

There is a first aid station at the Zoo, located at the Security office at the main entrance, but always come prepared by packing a few Band-Aids, for those unexpected stumbles and falls. Little children always seem to be running from one place to the next and inevitably they trip and scrape knees and elbows. While this is not a major emergency, it always involves a lot of tears and a frantic search for a bathroom to wash the wound and stop the bleeding. Band-Aids have magical powers for little ones. They stop the waterworks. Be sure to buy the kind with decorations on them—often cartoon characters that seem to possess powerful healing abilities.

Age of grandchild: toddler to teenager

Best season: Spring or early summer when there are lots of baby animals to see

Contact: 2300 Steele Street, Denver, CO 80205-4899 • (303) 376-4800; Fax: (303) 376-4801 • www.denverzoo.org

Also check out:

Cheyenne Mountain Zoo, Colorado Springs; www.cmzoo.org

Colorado Wolf and Wildlife; www.wolfeducation.org

Pueblo Zoo: www.pueblozoo.org

They say genes skip generations. Maybe that's why grandparents find their grandchildren so likeable. Joan McIntosh

Denver Museum of Nature and Science

Dinosaurs fly above you. Exhibit rooms lure you from the spacious center area and streams of people look for inspiration and knowledge. A discovery room is designed to get children involved and curious. What is more basic to who we are and the world we live in than nature and science? This is all about the world around us, the planet we share, the history of life, and the role of people—the basic building blocks of knowledge and a rich life. It is all here at the Denver Museum of Nature and Science.

The Discovery Zone is a good place to go when the museum experience becomes too exhausting or overwhelming. All museums contain more than

any person can absorb in one visit and the desire to see everything can cloud the experience, causing us to become tired, impatient and irritated. The brain has its limits and that is why we return to places like this. This way, we'll retain more knowledge and the experience will be more satisfying.

In the Discovery Zone, professionals will help the children create tracks, make crafts, dig for fossils, and maybe even sing and act! There are storytellers, a curiosity lab, games, drums and a tornado simulator—all geared to give you and your grandchildren a better understanding, appreciation and learning experience.

Many exhibits fill the halls each year and part of the excitement comes from the new and temporary displays that bring ideas and exhibitions that add to the depth of the Museum's stories. These can be about many topics, just as the permanent exhibits tell about many things, from displays about the earth and the minerals that are in its rocks and mantle, to the wildlife and plants that inhabit the variety of landscapes from the desert to the Arctic.

You will learn from dioramas, specimens, model mines, animal skulls, prehistoric fossils and reconstructed models. The dinosaurs overhead on the ceiling helps us visualize the true meaning of the fossil record, and in this way, it helps us break down barriers; it helps apply the past to the present and learn from the lessons of earth's history and apply them to contemporary life.

Bonding and bridging:

Nothing overwhelms our minds the way numbers do—great numbers like millions and billions are not numbers we really comprehend. When we visit the dinosaurs, we talk about millions of years ago, when we explore the rocks and geology we are moving in to billions of years. All of these stories have numbers to give us a perception of time.

Meanwhile numbers serve us in science and exploration. Some philosophers and scientists claim that numbers are the true language of the universe and that they can help explain almost everything. But how often do we work with numbers when we are with our grandchildren?

None of us need to be Einstein or Newton or Greene or Hawkings—they understand math at a level that befuddles us, but mathematics are an essential for academic success for our grandchildren and when they notice our appreciation for numbers, they'll emulate it and want to learn more.

A word to the wise:

When walking and talking reach their natural conclusion there are still more options for your day at the Museum. The Planetarium is a wonderful way to see how big the universe is and to learn about the small, fragile planet we live on. Maybe it is the best way for all of us to see how important it is to take care of the little spacecraft called Earth. And then to see what is on the Earth, the IMAX often has programs about nature and the planet. It might be too much to include both of these activities in one visit, but both should be on your list for future explorations.

Age of grandchild: 5 and up

Best season: All, but particularly when it is too cold, too wet or too hot to be outside.

Contact: 2001 Colorado Blvd, Denver, CO 80205 • (303) 322-7009 • www.dmns.org

Also check out:

Discovery Science Center, Fort Collins: www.dcsm.org

Fiske Planetarium and Science Center, Colorado Springs: http://fiske.colorado.edu

Western Colorado Math and Science Center, Grand Junction: www.sithok.org

The simplest toy, one which even the youngest child can operate, is called a grandparent. SAM LEVENSON

Denver Firefighters Museum

All of us grandparents who grew up in urban areas remember the large brick or stone firehouse found in almost every neighborhood. At some point in our early years, many of us had a chance to visit the firehouse and meet the firemen who lived and worked there. Policemen and firemen have always inspired awe in children. We are taught that these people work hard to keep us safe.

Firefighters, however, have an additional aura because of their shiny, flashy red fire trucks.

Children today are in just as much awe of these people and their machines as we were, but they may not have many opportunities to visit a Fire Station and meet the inhabitants. The Denver Fire Museum is both a historical museum and a place for educating youth. Built in 1909, Denver Station One is a dark brick building, with the recognizable double doors that allowed the fire engine to speed away. Inside, there are lots of artifacts from the early days of firefighting in Denver that grandparents will enjoy seeing, but there are lots of newer displays, exhibits and activities that will inspire and excite the kids throughout the museum.

Probably one of the most fascinating aspects of Fire Station life is the fire pole which was used to get the firemen down from their second floor sleeping quarters as quickly as possible. To kids it just looks like a piece of playground equipment that adults got to use. Fire poles were first used in Chicago in 1878. They were made of wood and coated with paraffin to lessen friction. In 1883, brass poles were introduced. In this Museum the kids can try sliding on one of these, not from the second story, but high enough to get a sense of how it felt.

While grandparents admire the antique engines and other equipment, the kids can handle some hoses, pipe nozzles, and hydrant caps on a "touch and feel" table. They can also time themselves and see if they can put on jackets, boots, hats, and masks, slide down the pole and get on the truck in 45 seconds, a challenge they're sure to love. Up on the second floor is a special kid's activity area, where the Museum really shines, because not only are the activities fun, they truly teach the kids about fire safety. In fact, grandparents will probably learn a thing or two.

Bonding and bridging:

The safety and survival of our grandchildren is foremost in all our minds and whenever we can do something to help them learn ways of staying safe, we feel better. We want to teach them the dangers that exist, without creating irrational fears. We know children find fire enticing. They're drawn to it, just as moths are to flames and we want them to think of fire as something to be enjoyed around a campfire or in a fireplace, with adults present. In a Museum such as this one, we can combine education and cautionary lessons in ways that are both fun and practical. Demonstrate a drop and roll for the kids and they will be tickled and want to try it. You might involve their parents too in a discussion about planned escape routes in their home, in case of fire. Most of us never do this, preferring to believe that such a crisis will never occur.

A word to the wise:

Throughout the year there are special events for kids and families, but two activities are designed especially for toddlers. One is called "Firehouse Tales for Tots," offered on the first Wednesday of every month. This includes both a story related in some way to firefighters and a craft activity following the story. The second is called Wee Wednesdays and is a fire safety series formatted along the idea of a play date with other kids, but with an emphasis on teaching basic fire safety behavior to kids at the earliest possible age. The fact that many household fires are started unintentionally by children playing with matches should be all the incentive that you need for them to learn these lessons.

Age of grandchild: toddler to 10

Best season: All

Contacts: 1326 Tremont Place, Denver, CO • (303) 892-1436 • www.denverfirefightersmuseum.org

Also check out:

Dr. Lester R. Williams Firefighter Museum, Colorado Springs: www.fire-museum.com

Hose Company No. 3, Pueblo: www.pueblofire.org/museum.htm

Old Fire House No. 1—Children's Museum, Trinidad: www.santafetrailscenicandhistoricbyway.org/fhsmus.html

At age seven, children have as passionate a longing for creative interactions and learning as they earlier had for explorations of the world. Joseph Chilton Pearce, *The Magical Child*

State Capitol

We are a culture of symbols—religious, economic and political—and no structure is more symbolic of our democratic system than the State Capitol. The Colorado Capitol is modeled after the National Capitol and built from 1886 to 1901. It was designed by architect Elijah E. Myers, who designed three state capitol buildings. The very size and shape is sure to let your grandchild know that something special should happen here.

This is not the only Capitol building that Colorado has had. First there was Colorado City, now part of Colorado Springs and then Golden. But Denver was still the hub for commerce and even before Denver became the official capital, many of the important issues were settled and documents were signed there.

Following the Civil War the new capitols became monuments to the national government. Even the streets around the Denver capitol have names that are familiar to Washington D.C.

Explore the Capitol grounds with your grandchildren and look for stories—like the pillars along the west entrance carved to depict early Denver. The tall entrance doors have early nineteenth-century light posts.

Inside there is a collection of paintings of all the U.S. presidents, and the massive stained glass dome honors the 15 men and one women who are each famous Coloradoans. For rock collectors, the Colorado rose onyx, the Yule Creek marble, and other magnificent colored stones make a beautiful building. The polishing of the stones took six years to complete and their beauty continues to dazzle visitors.

It is hard not to be impressed by a building that incorporates so much power and wealth, and your grandchildren will be overwhelmed by the dome, the large scale art, the open stairways, the center rotunda and the paintings of past governors.

Look into the chambers where laws are passed, go into the galleries if they are in session and watch the process from the balcony. Stroll the halls, find your Senator and go next door and find your Representative. You can wander on your own, but there are regular tours given every day.

Bonding and bridging:

The lesson you can impart from your own history is that it is the people who can make a difference in this country. The building is, in essence, yours. These are your employees and it is your responsibility to make sure they are doing a good job or you vote them out. Is there any more important lesson we can impart to our grandchildren? Democracy works only when individuals make their voice heard. Talk about how we elect people and what we do to try to make sure that each person has a voice. They must know the honor of voting is theirs and the responsibility to vote is everyone's.

Ask your grandchildren what they think is important and help them draft a letter to their Senator or Representative. Show them how to participate in government.

A word to the wise:

Make an appointment to visit your Senator and Representative. Even if you know them at home, they look different in their offices. Get a photo taken. Be prepared with a few good questions so the conversation doesn't lag, but do not make this a lobbying visit. If they are not in a committee or session, they love to see their constituents—especially when you are not there to lobby or complain! And they especially like to see young people showing an interest in their government. Expect the office to provide your grandchildren with some nice souvenirs and then help them to understand what they got after you leave the office.

Age of grandchild: 12 and above

Best season: The most excitement and energy is when the legislature is in session—winter

Contact: 200 E Colfax Ave, Denver, CO 80203-1784 • Tour desk: (303) 866-2604 • www.colorado.gov

Also check out:

Colorado City log cabin capital: http://history.oldcolo.com

Historic Golden, The Loveland Block: http://gardnerhistory.com/downtown/downtown2.htm

Your local county and city government buildings

Denver Art Museum

Starting with the sculptures outside of the building (both the roof and the plaza) you find whimsy. In art your children can find a fairy-book world depicted in many creative ways, from the giant chair outside the museum, where you can feel like Thumbelina, to the crazy boat of characters on the roof with arrows in their hats. We know of one grandmother who uses an art museum as a treasure hunt. They begin with a goal—horses, apples, arrows, goats… you name it. Then they go in to the collections looking for these objects and find out how many ways they are used. The children examine the

art. The sense of wonder is reinforced by the excitement of the hunt and the result is a child who is aware of the art, comfortable in the museum, and a potential art lover of the future.

The Denver Art Museum is spacious and invites exploration. One way they help you explore is with their family backpack, which gives the visit a feeling of a game. These can be checked out for a different adventure on each visit. There are also mobile kid activities on carts that can be found in different locations throughout the Museum. They are filled with interactive experiences. Or you can do an "art tube"—small activities that are in the galleries and involve a variety of art creations. A brochure will help you find each day's free activities and a children's area is designed to help promising art lovers.

There are many excellent collections like the African Art collection which demonstrates the creativity and the culture of a region. These are wonderful stories told in many dimensions. American Indian Art crosses the plains and the mountains and features a diversity of objects from totem poles to beadwork, all beautiful renditions that reflect the portion of the nation where indigenous groups lived.

For a flavor of the Old West and the life of the cowboy, mountain man, and settler, you will find dramatic and poignant stories in the Western Art Collection. Here are famous American artists like Russell and Catlin and Remington who lived the art they present. It is as close as we can get to a window into that part of our history. No matter what you choose to explore, the Denver Art Museum has a family-friendly feeling that has gained fame and recognition.

Bonding and bridging:

All kids like to color, and as we grow up we draw, play music, quilt, needlepoint, build in the wood-shop, restore or customize cars, enjoy films, take photos, build sand castles and create new ideas. All of this is art, but we don't label it that. People think art is something foreign, something "highbrow." But look around at the posters for concerts, films, church dinners—we use illustration and art to tell our stories. Help your grandchild see art all around them. Help them to realize how much our world depends upon art and how much the things we do each day would change if we did not encourage our creative ideas.

Start by coloring with them when they are young. Challenge them to try things, to find things in the pictures, in the house, and in the museums. Help them to look closer so they can develop a sense of art and observation.

A word to the wise:

Just remember there is too much to see in any one visit. There is no rule that says you have to see everything in the Museum. Nothing can spoil the desire to return more than boredom. See the things that spark interest, avoid those that don't. If this is for your grandchildren, then let their interest be the determining factor. You can encourage them to see some new things, but if you force them, you will create resentment rather than inspiration. Pick special shows you know will be of interest to them and take them when they are ready. It is hard to put an age on this event because it depends upon the child's maturity level.

Age of grandchild: 4 and up

Best season: All

Contact: Denver Art Museum, 100 W 14th Ave Pky, Denver, CO 80204 • (720) 865-5000 • www.denverartmuseum.org

Also check out:

Aspen Art Museum: www.aspenartmuseum.org

Boulder Museum of Contemporary Art: www.bmoca.org

Fine Arts Center, Colorado Springs: www.csfineartscenter.org

Museum of Outdoor Art, Englewood: www.fine-art.com

Museo de las Americas, Denver: www.museo.org

Our children grow up so fast. Maybe grandchildren are God's way of giving us a second chance at participating in the miracle of life. Unknown

55

Colorado History Museum

What would be a better location for a History Museum than near the capitol, where history is made every day and across the street from the library where history is available to the public? The Colorado Historical Society maintains a dynamic and engaging museum that brings the artifacts of history together with outstanding graphics and exhibits to allow us to engage with the story of Colorado.

Like all great museums, the History Museum features a variety of temporary exhibits that are available for short periods. The state's history is too complex to tell in just one exhibit, or just one visit, so check their website for the current topics and plan a visit accordingly.

Beginning with the bison statue in the courtyard, you are in for time-travel; the Museum is filled with images, artifacts, colors, sounds, movies, and objects to touch, feel, and explore. Leaving the ticket desk in the quiet upper level, you will descend into an abundance of stagecoaches and automobiles, mines and Indian teepees. Since exhibits change, the story gets more complex with every visit. There might be a story of Indian women in the West, the way people settled on different landscapes, or discussions about how ranchers and miners, explorers and pioneers used the land in a variety of ways to make their living. All around you, stories unfold in dioramas and realistic re-creations. To get multiple visual perspectives, walk the floor and climb the ramps.

TimeScape is a laser-lighted stage production which covers 10,000 years of Colorado's history, lasting one minute for every 1000 years. Through this exhibit, land and people are tied together.

There is something at the Museum for everyone. There are bound to be items that grandparents can relate to, as well as objects that will fascinate the grandchildren. Be prepared to move from exhibit to exhibit, until the initial energy is over, then settle in on a few exhibits and learn together.

Bonding and bridging:

How many of us remember yawning in history class or daydreaming when that subject came up? This generation of grandchildren is no different than we were, but a good museum can create excitement and curiosity about the past in a way that the classroom never can.

Every one of us has a personal history and when it's personal, it is always more interesting. Talk with your grandchildren about events that have been important to them. Was it the first day of school, the holidays, or a house they moved to? Then tell them some of the important parts of your history, but not so many that their eyes glaze over. Encourage them to write about their daily lives—whether in a diary or journal, or in emails to you—which you print out and save for them. One never knows how the events that we record today might someday be of interest to future generations. Talk to your grandchildren about making a family history museum. What would you put in it?

A word to the wise:

The Museum helps connect families to history with their "Let's Make History" weekend program. Activities for all ages allow participants to actually handle artifacts, learn skills, and see how experts perform their crafts each Saturday from 11 a.m. to 3 p.m. Check the website to see what is offered—it might be role playing or even song and dance. Letting the Museum staff lead the activity allows you to interact with your grandchild and help them to succeed and learn.

Age of grandchild: 5 and up

Best season: All

Contact: 1300 Broadway, Denver, CO 80203 • (303) 866-3682
• www.colorado.com/Listing.aspx?did=2062

Also check out:

Black American West Museum: www.blackamericanwestmuseum.com

Byers Evans House: www.colorado.com/Listing.aspx?did=2943

Pro Rodeo Hall of Fame, Colorado Springs: www.prorodeohalloffame.com

Ute Indian Museum: www.colorado.com/Listing.aspx?did=2815

Denver Botanic Gardens

At the Denver Botanic Garden there are so many interesting and unique gardens that it is hard to know where to go first. Spread over 23 acres, it is a treasure for all Coloradoans. But the designers chose to put their Children's Garden right near the entrance. For some people this may be all you can do on your first visit. The entry is graced by an arch with colorful glass-blown insects mounted on it and the first plantings you come to focus on the senses of touch, smell and taste. Here children are encouraged to rub the leaves and sniff the aroma that wafts up. During the growing seasons there will be some vegetables that they can nibble—with adult supervision, of course.

As you follow the path in this long, narrow space, you will come upon a digging area, equipped with shovels, hoes, and trowels. This is not a sandbox, but actual dirt that the kids can dig in, so if they are wearing special,

"can't get dirty" clothing, you may want to direct them past this spot. But this is the kind of activity that little kids love because it makes them feel like grown-ups. There are also sculptures that make sounds when the kids manipulate them and a maze made with vegetables growing in pots.

If you decide to explore more of the Garden, you will have lots of paths to choose from, and don't be surprised if the grandkids want to run ahead and see what is around the next hedge or corner. There are over 32,000 plants and water elements to see. Just think of all that oxygen being released around you.

This Botanic Garden also believes in displaying art alongside plants, and throughout the year there are rotating shows of sculpture and paintings scattered throughout and along the paths.

If the weather is wet or cold, you can still enjoy a visit by spending time in the Tropical Conservatory with its jungle-like, lush vegetation, high humidity, running water and pools with fish swimming slowly around. A tall, artificial ficus rises up toward the ceiling with steps you can climb for an overview of all that is growing below. In another room is an example of a cloud forest tree, bearing epiphytic (air) plants.

Bonding and bridging:

A visit to this Garden is a great way to introduce your grandchildren to the specific climatic and environmental conditions of their state. It is both an arid and alpine state and there are specific plants that grow best under these conditions. Spend some time by the Water Smart Garden, since water is a critical resource for both people and plants and discuss (especially with the older grandchild) how we can all conserve more and still have beauty growing around us.

If at all possible, begin taking your grandchildren to the Botanic Garden when they are still in their strollers. Expose them to the sights and soothing sounds of a place dedicated to growing things. For toddlers, every living thing is fascinating; they are ready and willing to be thrilled by the new smells and textures that the Garden incorporates. A garden, by its very nature, is a place of quiet and slow-paced life. We need to slow down and pay attention to the little details of life. Here you can help your grandchildren focus on the incredible mystery of flowers—their delicate scents and fragile petals.

A word to the wise:

There are many special events at the Gardens throughout the year. At the Denver Garden during the winter holiday season, the color comes from one million lights that sparkle in the darkness. This creates a magical feeling as you wander along the paths bundled against the cold. In Chatfield, where there is another branch of the Denver Botanic Garden, autumn brings the annual Pumpkin Festival and a corn maze where kids gleefully race through the course. Check the Botanic Garden website for upcoming events and visit in every season.

Age of grandchild: toddler to teenager

Best season: Any

Contact: 1005 York Street, Denver, CO 80206 • (720) 865-3500 • www.botanicgardens.org

Also check out:

Shambhala Botanic Gardens, Denver: www.shambhalamountain.org/gardens

The Gardens on Spring Creek, Fort Collins: www.fcgov.com/horticulture

Western Botanic Gardens, Grand Junction: www.wcbotanic.org

www.botanicgardens.org/content/our-gardens-chatfield-location

Wings Over the Rockies Air and Space Museum

There is something about flying that stirs our souls and our imaginations. We become bird watchers out of envy for the freedom of our avian friends. We have flying dreams that are memorable above all others. And we have pursued flight by extravagant means from the beginning of time. So, is it any wonder that this wonderful collection of early airplanes to space flight vehicles and displays is such a great hit with people of all ages?

The Museum is actually an historic, 1930s era Air Force hangar that has been decommissioned, so it's not surprising to find most of the aircraft displayed are Air Force planes. The hangar has 40,000 square feet to showcase the more than three dozen aircraft and space vehicles. It will take some time to walk past and around all of these flying machines, and be sure to look up to see some that are suspended above you.

Other parts of the building house the Spacecraft and Rocketry Technology exhibit, which will be of more interest to the older grandchildren, since they have some knowledge of what is out in space and have grown up knowing about the Shuttle and International Space Station. There are parts of the Apollo Command Module and a Titan IV rocket to check out, and another mockup of a space station module.

On the second Saturday of each month, from 10 a.m.–2 p.m., there is a special hands-on atmosphere that all ages will enjoy. On this day, you and your grandkids can climb into the cockpits of different airplanes and pretend for a moment that you are about to take off. For some grandparents this may be a very vivid memory. For the smaller grandchildren there is a chance to climb into the collection of toy pedal planes and taxi around. In addition, one day between Christmas and New Year's, the Museum has a special day that focuses on kids and includes lots of hands-on activities with an aviation theme. Build balsa planes or foam rockets, and spend time in the computer flight simulator labs. A Kid's Space designed for the pre-kindergarten child has tables set up with items they can manipulate or create.

Bonding and bridging:

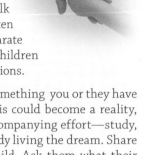

Dreams—both those we have at night and during our waking hours—can have an impact on our lives. Have you ever had a dream where you felt that you were actually flying? Has your grandchild? We can talk about what that might mean and why some frighten us, while others give us pleasure. We need to separate dreams from reality, but allow for our grandchildren to hold dreams about their future and their aspirations.

What about our daydreams? Is flying an airplane something you or they have dreamed about doing? For your grandchildren, this could become a reality, but as with any such dream, there has to be an accompanying effort—study, saving money or working with others who are already living the dream. Share with your grandchildren a dream you had as a child. Ask them what their dream for their future might be, and then let them know that dreams do come true, for those who hold on to them and help bring them to life. Charles Lindbergh's dream of flying across the Atlantic and the dream of flight for two bicycle makers with the last name Wright are wonderful examples of how dreams can get wings.

A word to the wise:

It is easy to get caught up in the dramatic shape of the military jets and the exotic adventure of space exploration, but help your grandchildren experience the wonder of the early forms of flight as well. Build their knowledge by making a model plane or flying a kite. Our grandchildren love the simple balsa gliders. There are so many models available, from these simple little planes to elaborate radio controlled airplanes. Choose the one that fits your budget and your interest and follow up on this flight of fancy.

Age of grandchild: 3 to teenager

Best season: Any

Contact: 7711 E. Academy Blvd., Denver, CO • 80230 • (303) 360-5360
• www.WingsMuseum.org

Also check out:

Peterson Air and Space Museum, Colorado Springs: www.petemuseum.org

Pueblo Weisbrod Aircraft Museum, Pueblo: www.pwam.org

The Spirit of Flight Center, Lafayette: www.spiritofflight.com

It is not a slight thing when they who are so fresh from God, love us. CHARLES DICKENS

Kit Carson County Carousel

This is one historical monument that is guaranteed to please the children—but truth in advertising requires us to admit—Kit Carson never rode on this carousel. However, there are many other prominent people in Colorado and across the nation who probably have or wished that they had. The Carousel is part of our historic past dating back to the gaslight era and this is the number one historical carousel in the U.S.A!

The merry-go-round name says it all, or perhaps we should say the Happy Go-Round. Because the imaginative motif of exotic animals and gaily painted horses that prance up and down has never failed to delight children and the ancient, antique and historic still have their magic.

Between 1885 and 1940 there were over 4,000 wooden carousels in the U.S., but today fewer than 150 of them are still in existence. Imagine the significance of these old timers—when we find them, we can delight in the excitement of our own parents and grandparents. When we extend the circle of happiness and life to our grandchildren, we are welcoming them to an extension of our own families and the delight of generations.

This magnificent carousel is housed in its own building and is part of each year's fair, but fortunately for visitors, you need not wait until the fair comes around. The museum and the ride are there for you to enjoy throughout the summer, and Carousel Number 6 of the 74 built by the Philadelphia Toboggan Company is still spreading joy.

Forty-six animals march to John Phillip Sousa. There is a giraffe with a snake twined around its neck, carvings of cupids, sheiks, medallions and even a gnome can be found if you enjoy the hide and seek of exploring the various carvings, as well as going for a ride. And if you do not like going up and down, there are four chariots with painted landscapes on their seat backs.

The carousel dates back to 1905 in Denver, but it is ageless and on each ride you are touching history.

Bonding and bridging:

Sharing an adventure is wonderful, but sharing the same adventure decades apart has to be one of the greatest of all experiences. Ask what the grandchildren like and then share what you liked when you rode a carousel at their age. There is no generational difference on a merry-go-round. Look at the paintings on the interior walls above the organ. Explore the animals and the elaborate designs. What is it that makes this so special for all generations?

What are the other things that you had in your life that your grandchildren can now experience—trains, horse rides, etc?

A word to the wise:

What is a carousel? A merry-go-round? Why the music, why the animals? How is it made? What is its history? This is a real story of Americana, but it is seldom told well like it is here. Invest some time in this small exhibit and you will learn even more than your grandchildren.

It might be the beginning of a quest to find and ride the best carousels still in existence and, by the way, grandparents ride too! Watching someone else do something is not the same as sharing the experience. So look at the carousel museum together and ride the ride together too!

Age of grandchild: 2 to10

Best season: Summer

Contact: Kit Carson Carousel, PO Box 28, Stratton, CO 80836
• 719-348-5562 • www.kitcarsoncountycarousel.com

Also check out:

Cheyenne Mountain Zoo.; a two row, 20 horse carousel built in 1925; part of the 1932 World's Fair: (719) 633-9925

Elitch Gardens, Denver; 1927 replacement for the Kit Carson Merry-Go-Round and now is historic: www.elitchgardens.com

Lakeside Amusement Park, 4601 Sheridan Blvd, Denver, Colo 80212; a 1909 three level platform from the Kansas Colonel—Charles Parker. One of 16 still in existence: (303) 477-1621

Santa's Workshop, Cascade; built in 1920

Forget not that the earth delights to feel your bare feet, and the winds long to play with your hair. KAHLIL GIBRAN

Bent's Old Fort and the Santa Fe Trail

Many people have the impression that Colorado is all mountains and mines. The image of the state and its history often features high peaks and deep valleys, but if you do not help your grandchildren correct this view they will be missing some of the legendary stories of the nation and the state.

The Santa Fe Trail is part of our national trail system that connects parks and historic sites from Missouri to New Mexico, and tells stories of Indians, Mexicans, and black and white Americans on the prairies and plains. One portion—the Cimarron Route—only touches the southeast corner of the state, but the Mountain Route crosses a big swath of Colorado following Highway 50 as it enters the state and then 350 as it exits.

No place captures the history better than Bent's Old Fort—an adobe structure that stands like a castle in the grass. This early outpost sat along the Arkansas River, the border with Mexico and later the Republic of Texas, prior to the U.S. victory in the Mexican War. Set back from the parking lot, it is a hot walk to the Fort, an appropriate way to enter this historic spot. The wagons, Indians, cavalry, trappers, and migrants all suffered heat and dry air in this area during the summer and cold and brutal winds in the winter. Even famous mountain men like Kit Carson and Thomas Fitzpatrick took comfort at the Fort.

But this was not a military post; it was truly a trading post built by Bent, St. Vrain and Company traders. You can walk into the rooms, see how they lived, walk the trade and warehouse rooms and see early commerce on the plains, visit the blacksmith shop and carpenter's rooms, or stroll into the opulently outfitted dining room where guests were entertained and the smellier traders and trappers were excluded.

There was even the first billiard room in the west, but the grandchildren might enjoy going up and down the stairs and walking the upstairs veranda to get a bird's eye view of the Fort and the surrounding landscape, or seeing the livestock that lives beside the Fort. There will be fires, even on hot days, for doing work and cooking meals. Costumed characters will occasionally show up and bring the kind of excitement that greeted all new arrivals at this remote site. Granddaughters can relate to the fate of 18-year-old Susan Magoffin who grew ill on the trail and recovered here in the best accommodations that the Fort had to offer.

Bonding and bridging:

There are many ideas for grandparents to explore here. This was the shopping center of the high plains, a trading post filled with all that anyone could want. Can you explain that to your grandchildren when they see the simple items that were being sold? Can you help them understand that commerce was not always in dollars, but rather in skins and meat? Would they trade a buffalo robe for hawk bells, beads, and abalone shells?

They can also explore how the various cultures survived and respected one another. William Bent had a Cheyenne wife and Charles Bent had a Mexican wife. But despite the Bent brothers' efforts, the military carried out the will of the government and took over portions of the Fort during the war with Mexico. The military also carried out "peace" talks while looking to invade and remove the Indians from their land, where they had always lived. Time, economics, warfare, cultural clashes are all brought together here in this remote and historic site where peace reigned for most of its existence.

A word to the wise:

Since you have traveled highways to explore this site, perhaps you could choose to follow portions of the original route. The same conditions that invited highway engineers attracted the wagon trains. The following sites are places in Colorado to get more perspective on the Santa Fe Trail. Trinidad has many historic brick buildings and celebrates Santa Fe Days each June. La Junta has the Otero museum complex with many old buildings, in addition to the museum collection. You can also visit Iron Springs and the Kit Carson Museum in Las Animas.

Age of grandchild: 6 and up

Best season: Avoid the hottest part of summer

Contact: Bent's Old Fort National Historic Site, 35110 Highway 194 East, La Junta, CO 81050-9523 • (719) 383-5010 • www.nps.gov/beol

Also check out:

Comanche National Grasslands: www.fs.fed.us/r2/psicc/coma

Santa Fe National Trail, National Park Service: www.nps.gov/safe

Santa Fe Trail Scenic Byway: www.santafetrailco.com

I like to walk with Grandpa, his steps are short like mine.
He doesn't say, "Now hurry up." He always takes his time. UNKNOWN

65

Pro Rodeo Hall of Fame

Is there a stronger image of the Old West than the cowboy on a bronco? The American West has long been more myth than reality, but the cowboy has continued to be the one true image that survives the movie, radio, television, books, and music. This is because the cowboy does not need exaggeration; he is the working man and the relationship he has with his horse, the cattle and the range makes for exceptional images, all of which come together in the rodeo.

Just catch a glimpse of the statue of Casey Tibbs, the superhero of the rodeo on the famed saddle bronc Necktie and you will want to come inside and see the people and pageantry that make up rodeo around the world. Grandchildren will love the color and the sound of the rodeo announcer that echoes among the exhibits. We found ourselves spending much more time exploring and learning than we intended because of the exhibits and the stories; like Bill Pickett who perfected steer wrestling in the 1800s by charging a long horn on his horse, jumping off in front of the beast, biting its lip and twisting the steer to the ground, a practice no longer allowed.

Have your grandchildren begin with the introductory film and then the colorful exhibit of clothes and gear through the ages, and observe how each cowboy uses clothing to create his own image as you view the individual inductee's trophy cases. Each cowboy has a display of boots, chaps, hats, saddles or anything else that helps identify them. You can talk about why they liked big buckles, what the spurs are for and why they wore chaps.

The Hall has animals as members too! How many sports Halls of Fame have animals on a par with human stars? So what makes these animals unique? How does an animal become a legend? Over the years we have had horses like "My friend Flicka," "Fury," "Black Stallion," and cowboys have shared their movie stardom with Silver, Trigger, and Champion, but rodeo animals are working stock and sometimes refuse to be ridden. Check out the bull Red Rock who refused to be ridden 309 times—he was a superstar with horns.

Bonding and bridging:

What many call the only real "American Sport" began July 4, 1869 when a group of bragging cowboys took their skills to a bronc riding contest, with the winner getting a new suit of clothes.

For many of our grandchildren life on the range, the ranch, and life on the horse is lost. Westerns are no longer the common fare on television or in the movies. But people who have worked with animals have a special understanding of animal strength and personality. Dogsledders in the north (and in the snow covered mountains), farmers, cowboys, and ranchers, zookeepers, wildlife researchers, all have a richer life because of the animals.

How did we learn to live and work with animals? Can you research this together? When you do, check out the rodeo events and see what parts of ranch life each event represents. This sport is also history. How does it differ from horse racing and show horses? There is a lot to talk about.

A word to the wise:

Do not miss the garden. Wonderful lifelike statues are placed around an outdoor garden and each pose is worth a longer look, not just because of the fine details, but because they are really stories frozen in motion and waiting for you to decipher with your grandchildren. Take your time to think up the stories together. Let your grandchildren tell you what they see in each bronze. Then you can walk back to the mini-rodeo corrals and, if you are lucky and have checked ahead of time, you might actually see someone performing one of the rodeo skills. And if not, there may be some livestock that your grandchildren can see.

Age of grandchild: 6 and up depending on their rodeo interest

Best season: All

Contact: Rodeo Hall of Fame & Museum, 101 Pro Rodeo Dr, Colorado Springs, CO 80919 • (719) 528-4764 • www.prorodeohalloffame.com

Also check out:

Black American West Museum: www.blackamericanwestmuseum.com

Colorado History Museum:
www.coloradohistory.org/hist_sites/CHM/Colorado_History_Museum.htm

Frontier Days Cheyenne, WY: www.cfdrodeo.com

All things are connected, like the blood which connects one family. Whatever befalls the earth befalls the children of the earth. CHIEF SEATTLE

67

Garden of the Gods

The red rocks rise out of the ground as if they sprouted like mushrooms after a rainy day, but these massive spires and ridges of sandstone are actually the remains of ancient seabeds, laid down 300 million years ago. Once the Earth's crust began to bend, crack and rise in the formation of nearby Pike's Peak, so too did this area, lifting and exposing layers of sediment that contain plant, marine and even dinosaur fossils.

People have been visiting this area long before the arrival of European settlers. Archaeologists have found evidence of humans here from as long as 3,400 years ago. And the native Ute people were still living in the area in the winter months into the 1870s. In the mid-to-late 1800s, explorers, gold seekers, and finally settlers, began to arrive in the region and they, too, were drawn to this marvelous geologic site. A couple of these early arrivals were surveyors. One saw the area and proclaimed that it would make a great spot for a beer garden, but his companion wisely recognized the uniqueness and beauty of the area and declared that it was better suited to be a "garden of the gods," and it has been called this ever since. It exists as a free, open space, owned by the City of Colorado Springs, due to the generosity and foresight of Charles Perkins who bought 480 acres of this land in 1879 with the intent to build a home here, but he decided it was just too beautiful to do so and decided to donate the land to the city for a public park. He died before he accomplished this act, but his children followed through on their father's wish and so today we and our grandchildren can walk through and enjoy this rocky garden.

A Visitor Center with informational exhibits and programming throughout the year is located across the road from the Park. You can drive through, bike, or ride horses in the park, but we recommend getting out and walking the paved paths that wind through and around the soaring stones. It's hard to stay on the path though, when this natural playground beckons. We couldn't keep our 18-month old grandson Ryan from climbing on the smooth, low boulders next to the path. The plants and animals in this garden are also unique because this is where three distinct biomes—grassland, pinon-juniper woodlands and mountain forest meet. It is also a place where peregrine falcons soar around the peaks of the formations. The red of the rocks against the deep blue sky are the most dramatic colors in this garden.

Bonding and bridging:

A park like this gives us an opportunity to talk with our grandchildren about philanthropy and how the generosity and foresight of one individual can create so much good for so many. Ask your grandchildren what they think would have happened to this land if Charles Perkins hadn't given it to the city. Looking not far beyond the park borders, you can see the houses creeping up the hillsides. They built homes here because it is beautiful and their homes are worth more because the park makes them more valuable. If this were filled with homes would it be as valuable to the city? To everyone? We need to reflect on how much parks mean to all of us.

It is also a good place to talk about change. What is permanent and what isn't? Even these rocks are changing every year as the rain, wind and snow slowly gnaw away at their surface. We can't see the changes because our lifetimes are just not long enough, but they are changing just the same. We too are changing, every day, and our experience, what we value, what we look like and how we think, will not be the same five to ten years from now.

A word to the wise:

The temptation to climb on these rocks is great and you will see people in climbing gear doing just that, but it is illegal to climb or even rock scramble in the park without permission to do so. There are many signs warning people of this danger and the rules. If your grandchildren are enticed by the climbing potential, check with one of the local sport climbing businesses and schedule a lesson for them. You might also spend some time watching a class that is in session or other climbers. If possible, talk to some of the climbers and let your grandchild ask them questions about their sport.

Age of grandchild: toddler to teenager

Best season: Spring

Contact: 1805 N 30th Street (at Gateway Rd.), Colorado Springs, CO 80904
• (719) 634-6666 • www.gardenofgods.com/home/index.cfm?&Flash=1

Also check out:

Canyons of SE Colorado: www.springfieldcolorado.com/canyons.html

Colorado National Monument, Grand Junction: www.nps.gov/colm

Roxborough State Park, Denver: parks.state.co.us/Parks/Roxborough

Never have children, only grandchildren. Gore Vidal

Cheyenne Mountain Zoo

You might say all zoos are alike in terms of the animal species exhibited, but there is one quality of the Cheyenne Mountain Zoo that sets it apart from all others. It's built on the side of a mountain, sitting 6,800 feet above sea level! It's worth a visit simply for the fantastic views of the city and eastern plain spread out below. This zoo, which opened in the 1930s, is well worth a visit for its animal exhibits too.

After entering through the terra cotta plaza, the first exhibit will delight everyone. Who can resist giraffes, these gentle giants of the African plains? This herd is the largest of any zoo and because of the elevated walkway, you are nearly eye level with them. While public feeding of animals at the Zoo is not allowed, an exception is made at this exhibit, where you can purchase special crackers to feed the giraffes. Adults and children alike eagerly offer treats to the animals who are equally eager to take them on their long (18-21 inches), indigo-colored tongues. Also in this African Rift Valley section of the Zoo there are zebras, meerkats, colobus monkeys and warthogs.

The zoo recently completed the Rocky Mountain Wild exhibit—a three-acre space. Here you can see some of the larger mammals of the Rocky Mountain region, including the grizzly. Climb the newly-built fire tower to get a panoramic view of the zoo, as well as of bears as they forage below, looking for fish in their pool and other treats (planted by keepers) in a hollowed out, artificial tree.

Don't miss Primate World. Here you can see the gorillas, orangutans, and chimpanzees, as well as their smaller relatives, the siamangs and macaques. The gorillas have a large outdoor area, but in colder weather they are indoors. The similarities of these animals' bodies and eyes to our own, not to mention their genetic similarity, can be haunting. Their behavior reflects our own too, and all ages can spend a lot of time observing and being entertained by their antics, but also being challenged by their captivity.

For younger grandchildren there is My Big Backyard, which can be a welcome respite for grandparents. Climbing on giant lawn chairs and plants, getting close to free ranging chickens and petting some small farm animals are activities guaranteed to satisfy everyone.

Bonding and bridging:

The excitement of the children seeing these new, living creatures is contagious and you will remember the thrill you felt the first time you saw an elephant or a giraffe. The zoo gives us a chance to talk about nature and the animals that live in the wild. Why are some endangered? And what can we do to help them survive? You may get into a discussion with an older child about such issues as captivity. Is it right? If so, why? Then talk about the newer exhibits and what they like about them. Remind them that Zoos and the general public have only recently come to understand the needs certain animals have to live healthy lives. We can't really judge their happiness, though animals that reproduce in captivity generally indicate a better adjustment to their situation than those that don't. This is also a great chance to talk about how important it is for us to protect wild areas, so that these animals will always have a place to live in the wild, not in Zoos.

A word to the wise:

Because this Zoo is built on the side of a mountain, be prepared to walk uphill from one exhibit area to the next. The path winds its way up the slope, gaining 120 feet by the time you reach the Asian Highlands. If you're pushing a stroller, it will be even more of a workout, so you will have to adjust how much you see to your fitness level. If you or your grandchild needs a lift, there is a Tram; you can hop on and off (for a small fee). It makes a loop of the Zoo grounds every 15 minutes, but it only runs on weekends from Memorial to Labor Day.

Age of grandchild: toddler to teenager

Best season: Spring and Summer (when there are more baby animals)

Contact: 4250 Cheyenne Mountain Road, Colorado Springs, CO 80906 • (719) 633-9925 • www.cmzoo.org

Also check out:

Butterfly Pavilion and Insect Center: www.butterflies.org

Colorado Wolf and Wildlife: www.wolfeducation.org

Denver Zoo: www.denverzoo.org

Pueblo Zoo: www.pueblozoo.org

Grandparents, like heroes, are as necessary to a child's growth as vitamins. JOYCE ALLSTON

Buell Children's Museum and Sangre de Cristo Art Museum

Rated the number two Children's Art Museum in the nation by *Child Magazine*, this has to be part of your grandchild's experiences. From the inspired playfulness of the sculptures outside the Museum entrance, to the impish sculpture that bids you to leave the Children's Museum and explore the Art Museum, this is a place of mystery, magic and fun.

Our grandchildren loved the outdoor statues which began their journey into imagination, but if the excitement is too great and they want to get inside, visit the statues as you leave. The Children's Museum is found on two floors of a 12,000 square foot facility (the Art Museum is next door, but separate) and is geared for hands-on exploration and discovery. Be sure to let your grandchildren's imagination loose. Scattered throughout the museum are multi-sensory exhibits, sounds, videos and lights that are activated by fifty different sensors in the walls. Finding them is part of the fun. Children might get so intrigued with locating the buttons that they fail to comprehend the information.

The kids can watch a program or create their own theatrical masterpiece in the El Pomar Magic Carpet Theater. This exhibit usually includes an opportunity to try on different clothes and create costumes that aid in the child's construction of stories. Sometimes the Museum brings in costumed characters to interact with the children—check the schedule for dates and times.

Creative expression is encouraged at the Artrageous Studio which provides all the ribbon, paper, glue and equipment to develop one-of-a-kind works to take home. If the children are under four years old they can explore the Buell Baby Barn which is full of animal and farm toys. Some exhibits change, so check their website to see what is current.

We enjoyed sitting among the giant stuffed animals and reading books—a quiet activity that was a nice complement to the more ambitious activities that fill the remaining hours of the experience.

Bonding and bridging:

When you are with the children you are not only facilitating their activities, but also modeling behavior and interest. They will be interested in what you are interested in. When you ask them to draw, you might consider drawing too. Keep in mind that they are watching us all the time. When you show excitement it is a message for later in their life. They look at you as their ideal of adulthood. You are supporting them in ways you might never realize.

Talk about artists—how adults have taken their crayons and paints to advanced levels and make a living. Some paint buildings, others paint images, some draw lines in strange artistic designs and others design buildings. Some build pots and sculpture, others build buildings and bridges. Creativity can lead in many directions.

A word to the wise:

The Art Museum is a separate exhibit hall to visit when the children are ready for a quieter experience. But if they have engaged in some of the art activities in the Museum, they might like to walk through an exhibit. Allow them to find what they like and ask them why. What makes art? If they find a theme they like, talk about it and then return to the Children's Museum and help them capture the art in their own creation.

Age of grandchild: any age, but we recommend 3–10.

Best season: Any time you want to be inside

Contact: 210 N Santa Fe Avenue, Pueblo, CO 81003 • (719) 295-7200 • www.sdc-arts.org/bcc.html

Also check out:

Mountain Top Children's Museum, Breckenridge: www.mtntopmuseum.org

The Children's Museum of Denver: www.cmdenver.org

The Children's Museum of Durango: www.childsmuseum.org

WOW Children's Museum, Boulder: www.wowmuseum.com

Pike's Peak and the Cog Railroad

No doubt about it—the fourteeners (peaks over 14,000 feet) have a special allure in Colorado, which has 58 peaks in this rare air. These are the top peaks, the highest group south of Canada and they are a mix of challenges, shapes, and forms. But of all of them—Pike's Peak is probably the most famous and most universally known. It is the most visited mountain in the U.S. and the second most in the world (behind Mount Fuji).

Named for Zebulon Pike, this massive mountain rises in the Front Range, the barrier of mountains that form a wall behind the towns of Fort

Collins, Boulder, Denver, Colorado Springs and numerous other communities of the high plains. Because this complex of mountains comes up from the mountain high plateau of treeless plains, they seem even higher, and Pike's Peak is that much more dramatic because it hovers over the communities of Colorado Springs and Manitou Springs and is truly one of the giants.

Fortunately, there are a variety of ways to reach the top. For the really fit, there are hiking trails; for those who want wheels under them there is a steep mountain road with sharp drop-offs and hair pin curves that make it a colorful mountain drive. But for those who prefer a scenic route without hassle—there is the Cog Railroad.

The cog railroad ride takes you to 14,110 feet, the highest railroad in the U.S. It begins its 8.9-mile journey at the depot in Manitou Springs and then ascends through spruce, fir and Ponderosa pine followed by the strange and ancient bristlecone pines—the oldest trees in North America. There are cascades in the stream beside the train and views of mule deer, marmots, and bighorn sheep.

Cog railroads not only ascend steep grades, but they are unique in other ways—because there are no wheels and no steel tracks. Instead there is a central track that looks like one side of a zipper. It depends upon a cog wheel—a gear wheel that has teeth that mesh with the zipper and the train literally climbs the mountain!

Enjoy the top and start your personal list of fourteeners.

Bonding and bridging:

People are natural list makers. Bird watchers keep lists of birds seen in their lifetime, world birds, state birds, country birds, annual birds. Kayakers keep track of the streams and rapids run. Sports fans keep statistics and records from seasons, careers and leagues. We list the flowers in the garden, make lists to go to the grocery store, and create lists to send out cards. Our lives are ordered and compared by lists. So keep lists of things you do together or things you see together. Let your grandchildren see that you are making a list and let them contribute to it. Eventually you will want them to have the lists—they are another form of album.

Climbers keep track of their peaks and many people "bag" the fourteeners. Make this an occasion. Take peak photos with your own family flag. Record the day, the weather, the time and the people you are with. Bring along a flag, the U.S. flag or your own family or community flag for a photo and share with friends and family. And remember—Zebulon Pike never did make it to the top!

A word to the wise:

The elevation at the top comes as quite a surprise. When you ascend 9,000 feet in a short time your lungs cannot adjust. Your pulse and your breathing will labor to capture the oxygen you are conditioned to have. This can create shortness of breath or labored breathing and it can cause headaches. You need to be aware because your grandchildren may be experiencing this for the first time and not know what is happening. You usually don't spend much time at the top. Drink some water. Stay calm. When you descend your body will find its oxygen and you and they will feel better.

Age of grandchild: 5 and up

Best season: summer

Contact: Manitou & Pike's Peak Cog Railway, 515 Ruxton Ave, PO Box 351, Manitou Springs, CO 80829 • (719) 685-5401 • www.pikespeakcolorado.com; www.cograilway.com

Also check out:

The 14er's: http://www.14ers.com

Florissant Fossil Beds National Monument

As you wander down the trail at Florissant Fossil Beds National Monument, past grassy meadows and clusters of ponderosa pine trees, the warm, dry mountain air blows steadily. Stop for a moment and have your grandchildren close their eyes and try to imagine what this place looked and felt like 33 million years ago when it was a lush, moist land, covered with ferns, shrubs, giant redwoods, and cedar trees.

Then, when they open their eyes, have them look for one of the fossilized stumps that are scattered across this National Monument. You are looking at the remains of what was once a living giant that has been transformed into a type of rock—what we call petrified wood. Have them picture volcanoes with mud flowing down their sides (Lahars) which create natural dams by stopping the flow of rivers and creating lakes. A mudflow buried these trees, (some were 230 feet tall and 38 feet around), and gradually led to their current condition. Fine volcanic ash fell and settled in the lakes and covered insects and plant material causing their fossilization.

This Monument is a wonderful natural area with 14 miles of hiking trails and a paleontologist's dream. These 6,000 acres have some of the most diverse and rich deposits of plant and insect fossils in the world. More than 140 species of plants have been identified and over 1,400 species of insects. Most of the plants that existed here no longer live in Colorado. The insects were similar to those found somewhere in the world today such as the African tsetse fly.

The Visitor Center has brochures and guides for your walks. If you don't have the time or ability to do the 1.4-mile Petrified Forest Loop, you can visit the exhibit just behind the Visitor Center. You'll notice there are railings around all the stumps and a roof overhead. These have been put in place to protect the fossils from the weather, and from unscrupulous visitors who would take pieces of the trees as souvenirs.

Elk and mule deer graze in the grasses and coyotes, fox, bears and mountain lions hunt the herbivores. Smaller mammals include the ground squirrels, porcupines, and birds. Be on the lookout for Albert's squirrel. It is black, with tasseled ears and it depends on Ponderosa pine to survive.

Bonding and bridging:

When we think about a dramatic event like a lahar (mudslide), we sometimes think nothing like that could happen again, but there was a lahar associated with Mount St. Helen, and terrible lahars in southeast Asia recently. The story of this place is not just the fossils and an ancient time in Colorado, but also the forces of climate and geology. When we strip trees from a mountain side we increase the potential for a lahar. We do not want to give our grandchildren nightmares; we want to inform them.

The Monument has a policy of controlled burns each winter. With the arrival of settlers to this area, the landscape changed, due to agriculture and forestry practices, one of which was fire suppression. But this is a land that had long known natural fires (through lightning). The Park Service has learned that to maintain the plant communities, there must be periodic fire. It is a difficult and complex concept for kids—that fire can be good. But it is an example of how new knowledge can shape behavior.

A word to the wise:

Looking at all the fragments lying around, it is tempting to pick up a few to take home, but it is illegal to remove any pieces of petrified wood from the Monument. What remains today is just a fragment of what once was present. When the area was discovered by settlers, they began taking samples with them as souvenirs. Walt Disney purchased an entire stump in 1956 for Frontierland at Disneyland. If everyone who visited the Monument were to collect just one piece, in time there would be nothing left for future visitors. This too is an important lesson for your grandchild.

Age of grandchild: 5 to teenager

Best season: Summer

Contact: PO Box 185, Florissant, CO 80816 • (719) 748-3253
• www.nps.gov/flfo/index.htm

Also check out:

Colorado Fossil Show, Denver: www.mzexpos.com/colorado_fossil.htm

Dinosaur Depot Museum, Canon City: www.dinosaurdepot.com

Dinosaur Journey Museum, Fruita:
www.dinosaurjourney.org/Westerncolorado.htm

Royal Gorge Bridge and Park

This is a grand canyon to be sure, but narrower than that of the Colorado River. This canyon has been created by the endless action of sand and pebbles carried by the Arkansas River as it ground its way through ancient granite and gneiss rock. At the narrowest point the walls of the Gorge are only 1250 feet apart. These rocky walls are the remains of ancient mountains from the pre-Cambrian era that have risen into peaks multiple times, and each time the rocks rose, the river cut through and the mountains eroded away, except for the present peaks.

When you come to this park, your attention is drawn downward. Typically, we humans have a natural inclination to look down into canyons with combined awe and fear. The Royal Gorge Bridge and Park highlights an incredible natural feature with a variety of ways to view the depths.

You can peer down from overlooks, walk the 1200 foot bridge and look over the sides to the river below, or take an incline railway to the bottom of the Gorge. You ride standing up in a contraption that looks like metal cages with the rock walls on either side. This tram was built in 1931 and is the world's steepest incline railroad, called such because the "car" moves on tracks down the 45 degree slope. It takes five and a half minutes to traverse the 1550 feet to the bottom. At the bottom, you can get out and can walk even farther down toward the river. If you're lucky, you may get to see some whitewater rafters or kayakers come shooting past.

If you or your grandchildren don't have a fear of heights and want a 360 degree view of the Gorge and the Sangre de Cristo Mountains, you can ride 1,178 feet above the Gorge in the candy red tram cars on suspended cables.

Amusement Park type rides at the Gorge include a small train for the younger ones, and a hair raising Skycoaster that you may not even wish to watch. Warning: teenage grandchildren may want to try it.

On the far side of the Bridge is a Wildlife Park where you can stroll on paths to view large mammals such as bison, elk, and bighorn sheep. This is a nice, adrenaline reducing activity after all of the other vertiginous ones.

Bonding and bridging:

The bridge was built in 1929. It is the highest suspension bridge in the world at 1178 feet above the Arkansas River. It is hard to imagine the skill and courage of those who put the steel beams in place, especially since we know that worker safety laws were pretty much nonexistent in that era! Yet the workers persevered and in five months the feat was accomplished. Many people take risks in their daily work, but we don't often appreciate their efforts. Police officers and fire fighters quickly come to mind, and there are people today who climb to great heights putting up cell and TV towers, as well as high rise buildings. We all take risks in our lives and it's important to share those you've taken with your grandchildren. Let them know how you felt, if you were frightened, but why you did it. They, too, will face many challenges and without the risk takers, progress will cease. We need to encourage them to evaluate situations and decide whether it is worth the risk or not.

A word to the wise:

There is another way to see the Gorge, from the bottom, and that is to take a train ride on the Royal Gorge Route Railroad. It is a 1950s era train, which is fun in itself. The ride begins in Canon City and travels for two hours through breathtaking scenery. You'll be craning your neck a lot looking up at the top of the Gorge, but there is always the wild and rushing river next to the train track to capture your attention.

Age of grandchild: 4 to teenager

Best season: Spring or Summer

Contact: 4218 County Road 3A, Cañon City, CO 81215 • (719) 275-7507; (888) 333-5597 • www.royalgorgebridge.com

Also check out:

Curecanti National Recreation Area: www.nps.gov/cure

Grand Canyon of the Gunnison: www.nps.gov/blca

Gunnison Gorge National Conservation Area: www.co.blm.gov/ggnca

Red Rock Canyon, Colorado Springs: www.springsgov.com/page.asp?navid=788

Royal Gorge, Canon City: www.canoncitycolorado.com

It's amazing how grandparents seem so young once you become one. UNKNOWN

Great Sand Dunes National Park

Try to imagine this: a sandbox and playpen 150,000 acres in size! It is 30 square miles of sand with dunes that rise 750 feet from their base to their crest. The main dune area is six miles wide by eight miles long. Now that is a play area! No wooden structure holds this sand. No playground surrounds it. No child has ever dug to the bottom of the pile, and no children have lacked the space for their own imagination to roam.

Sand Dunes is a park, a playground, and a nature preserve surrounded by the Sangre de Cristo mountains, a magnificent forested and snow-capped wall that makes a mighty nice fence for controlling the landscape and defining the park. And if sand is not enough, this land-locked dune formation also features

a shallow, wide stream perfect for wading, washing, cooling off and playing. No roaring rapids, no waterfalls, no deep spots, just a meltwater flow from the high mountaintops that might dry up in midsummer and during hot, dry years even before it reaches the main parking lot.

The park has a Visitor Center to help you understand how the sand got here and perhaps more importantly, why it stays. We do not know how old it is, but we think it is thousands, not millions, of years old and it might be a remnant of the feature called Lake Alamosa, a lake that is only visible in the imagination of geologists.

You are free to walk up into the dunes and should be prepared for crossing the creek in wet times of the year. Grandparents should concentrate on play and discovery rather than goals like reaching the summit of the highest dune. It is not only one mile to the first crests, it is sand you are walking on and sand is hard to climb.

Bring beach and sand toys to play with, bring plastic sheets, flat-bottomed plastic sleds, or snowboards to slide down the slopes, and enjoy the combination of experiences. When the children are ready, you can show them the plants and animals that surround the dunes.

Bonding and bridging:

While climbing the dunes can be a challenge for many of us, we can enjoy the view from the picnic area and the Visitor Center and play with our grandchildren at Medano Creek. In these locations the children can play in safety; nature provides all the tools for discovery and imagination. Our job is to challenge that imagination.

Does any question typify our grandchildren's mental growth more than the question—Why? Sometimes it seems there is no end to the word and no answer that will turn it off, but time may remove it from our daily experience and for some people it becomes lost. Foster it. Here is a mystery: Why are these dunes here? How old are they? Will they always be here? No one knows—isn't that nice? So we can speculate.

Asking 'why' is the first step in science, the basis for learning. The world is full of 'why' questions and it is fun to absorb them, learn what others are thinking, what ideas are most popular. It is good to know that there is more to know.

A word to the wise:

Even a big sand pile has dangers. You do not want to emphasize them, but you need to be aware. In the midsummer on cloudless days, the sand can heat up to 140 degrees. The best time to be out is the morning and the evening. None of us is equipped for desert heat, but we can be wise and avoid its power. Even if you do decide to go to the dunes in the best times of the day, bring water and watch out for dehydration. Wear shoes to protect against both heat and wear and tear!

Age of grandchild: All

Best season: Spring

Contact: Visitor Center, 11999 Highway 150, Mosca, CO 81146 • Main (719) 378-6300; Visitor Center (719) 378-6399 • www.nps.gov/grsa

Also check out:

Colorado National Monument: www.nps.gov/colm

Florissant Fossil Bed National Monument: www.nps.gov/flfo

Mesa Verde National Park: www.nps.gov/meve

Rocky Mountain National Park, Estes Park: www.estes-park.com

Alamosa and Monte Vista National Wildlife Refuges

Traveling west from the high plains, you cross over a mountain pass in the Sangre de Cristo Mountains and the high plains give way to the San Luis Valley, a flat plain 7,800 feet high which extends 100 miles north and south and 50 miles east west. Mount Blancs in the east soars to 14,345 feet and touches the clouds. Mountains peek at the rim of the valley in all directions.

To the north is the famous Sand Dunes National Park and the unique ecology of this stationary sand pile. Melting high country snow sends streams into the valley to replenish the aquifer and support marshes of cattails in two spectacular refuges—Alamosa and Monte Vista on the valley edge.

Alamosa is a combination of wet meadows, river oxbows and the flood plain of the Rio Grande, with dry uplands of greasewood and saltbush. The wild landscape of this refuge is best seen from a two-mile round-trip hiking trail. With luck you might find coyotes, beaver, mule deer, and birds of prey. Both songbirds and waterfowl are here as well, so keep your binoculars ready.

Monte Vista is a more managed landscape with dikes and water control structures determining the water levels and water distribution, but don't let that keep you from seeing the diversity and beauty of the patchwork wetlands. Thanks to the Refuge, the ditches of the 1800s have been replaced with ponds. Instead of taking the water from the land, it is retained so that it can feed the aquifer while helping waterbirds reproduce.

Bird watching is one of the most popular activities in the world, but it is hard for children to get started unless you find some simple starting points. One starting point is a bird feeder, where birds are close, slow and easy to observe, again and again. Another is a wildlife refuge like this, where the birds are concentrated in open water. They are not flighty, like warblers, and not hidden by branches or leaves, so your grandchildren can take the time to find and observe them.

Ducks, herons, avocets and other colorful, large birds help young ones relate to feathered animals. The loop road may even give you a chance to see an elk!

Bonding and bridging:

Animals are part of our lives: dogs, cats, caged birds, and fish in aquariums share our homes. They require care, which teaches our children a sense of responsibility and demonstrates that all life forms have personality, beauty, and importance. Pets also connect us with wild animals. Our dogs were once wild wolves that have changed through selective breeding. Lions, tigers, and pumas are large and wild, but they still are cats.

While we hunt, breed and slaughter animals and consume them for our benefit, they still deserve respect and should not be harmed or treated cruelly. We ask them to do work, pull our sleds, haul our loads, give us rides, provide us with milk, lay our eggs, and they in turn need care. Help your grandchildren make this connection.

A word to the wise:

In Nebraska, the concentration of Sandhill Cranes each November brings thousands of people to observe them along the Platte River. Near Michigan City, the eastern Sandhills cause celebration and busloads of observers. A western population of Sandhill Cranes uses Monte Vista as one of their staging areas. Both spring and fall, 20,000 cranes stop in for a visit and since 1983 they have been welcomed with a March festival. Join in for bird watching for raptors, waterfowl, and cranes, and enjoy the speakers and tours. So many people who care make the event more exciting and meaningful.

Age of grandchild: 3 and up

Best season: Spring

Contact: Alamosa National Wildlife Refuge • 9383 El Rancho Lane Alamosa, CO 81101 • (719) 589-4021 • http://alamosa.fws.gov

Also Check Out:

Arapaho NWR: www.fws.gov/arapaho
Baca NWR: www.fws.gov/alamosa/BacaNWR.html
Rocky Flats: www.fws.gov/rockyflats
Rocky Mountain Arsenal: www.fws.gov/rockymountainarsenal
Two Ponds: www.fws.gov/twoponds

Ghost Towns of Creede

Every child is captivated by ghosts at some point—whether it is Casper the Friendly Ghost on an old cartoon show or some modern cartoon version of ghosts with Scooby Doo. They see ghosts in movies and they eventually encounter adventurers like Indiana Jones or treasure hunters like the Pirates of the Caribbean. So capture that intrigue—go hunting for ghost towns. There are many ghost towns in Colorado, remnants of lost dreams, of fortune hunting, and the desire for new beginnings.

These are old buildings and pieces of the past strewn across a landscape that has been recaptured by nature after the ore, the dream, or the good weather played out. To most of us, the ghosts are only the winds blowing through the empty windows or the logs of old cabins. Yet the memories of the people are still here and maybe that is the real essence of ghosts.

A must stop for ghost hunters is Creede, a unique location. The town is set in the mountains on a curve just off the main route, but worth the time to explore. The history of this region is in the rocks, mines, and mountains and some of the best ghost ruins in the state. The road is its own adventure, and not just because it is steep. First there is an optical illusion that might be called an "obstacle" illusion. Leaving town to start out on the 17-mile loop you have to convince yourself that you are not just driving to the end of a dead-end road, or even worse, driving straight into the mountainside. Keep the faith, the rock wall will open, and you will be on your way. This is the Bachelor Mine Loop and one of the best historic drives in the Colorado mountains.

This is a town of Western history. In 1890 Nicholas Creede discovered a high-grade silver vein on Willow Creek, a tributary of the Rio Grande and a silver rush was on! The result was a boom camp with a temporary population of 10,000. The residents left just as quickly once the ore played out.

On the loop you will see Willow Creek, Equity Mine, and the old town site of Bachelor. A guide book will help you with the details and a sign gives you a good start, but more important than the facts are the feelings you get from this area. At the end of the loop be sure to visit the cemetery, where all illusions of wealth ultimately end.

Bonding and bridging:

What is wealth? Is it all the gold in the world or all the toys in the toy store? Why do people say, "money can't buy you happiness?" These buildings were put here by people with dreams; but not by people who cared about the future of the land and what they left behind; nor did they care about the Indians who were driven out of their land because of gold and silver.

Talk about the difference between want and need, about having a sense of place versus the decisions made by a lust for wealth. It is easy to clear forests, drill, or dig a mine when it is not our home that is being disturbed. What is the difference between power and respect? These are all important questions that will help your grandchildren plot their own future and make their own decisions.

A word to the wise:

Ghost towns are exciting to explore, but they are also dangerous. These structures are in a state of collapse. Floors can give way under weight. There is the possibility of broken glass, nails, and other sharp and dangerous items. Often they are on steep ground and near fast streams. You have to have control over your grandchildren and they should understand the risks and be responsive to your orders. In addition, in some old structures there could be rattlesnakes, scorpions and black widow spiders. This sounds like a list of horrors, but in fact the dangers are minimal—when the precautions are maximum. Be safe, curious, and respectful of the places. It is your responsibility to make sure that these fascinating places are not harmed by your actions, so that others can continue to visit and enjoy.

Age of grandchild: 5 and up

Best season: summer

Contact: Creede/Mineral County, Chamber of Commerce, P. O. Box 580, Creede, CO 81130 • (800) 327-2102 • www.creede.com/bachelor_loop.htm

Also check out:

Colorado Ghost Town Guide: www.coloradoghosttowns.com

Ghost Town Museum, Colorado Springs: www.ghosttownmuseum.com

St. Elmo, considered by some the best preserved ghost town: www.legendsofamerica.com/CP-StElmo1.html

I like to do nice things for my grandchildren—like buy them those toys I've always wanted to play with. Gene Perret

Black Canyon of the Gunnison National Park

Think about walking to the edge, any edge, and not knowing what lies beyond—it is mysterious, a little frightening and yet impossible not to look over and see what is there. The Black Canyon of the Gunnison is like that mystery. It is so deep—2,772 feet!—and so narrow, that you can only glimpse the bottom by venturing out on the vista locations that the National Park has created, which include walls to protect you from the dizzy effects of staring down into the black abyss.

The Grand Canyon is deeper, more colorful and wider, which gives it a special majesty, while the Black Canyon moves through dark igneous and metamorphic rocks that receive very little sunshine throughout the day.

Go to the Visitor Center to get grounded. Visit the overlooks or, if you have the ability, walk the Rim Rock Trail. As you gaze into the canyon, you can watch for the animals that live within these breathtaking views. Mountain bluebirds in the open lands, Steller's jays in the pines, canyon wrens and American dippers in the bottom and the amazing aerial specialists—peregrine falcons and white-throated swifts enjoying the heights and rocks.

Imagine the rocky earth bulging upward and the river cutting its way through. The power of water is dramatic here. The river moves through 48 miles of canyon (14 in the National Park) and is most dramatic and narrow in the park which contains 18 overlooks. The drop in water level from beginning to end of the National Park portion of the canyon is an average of 96 feet per mile—no wonder it moves so fast and has great power to erode. Within one stretch it actually drops 480 feet in two miles—that is like flowing down a playground slide!

Now the river is controlled by dams and erosion has slowed down, but there is still a danger each spring when the combination of rain and cold freezing nights can lead to dangerous conditions. For instance, on April 4, 2008, an avalanche sent a boulder weighing six million pounds into a road west of Crystal Dam, leaving a crater 100 feet across and 8 feet deep.

Bonding and bridging:

There are no bridges here, but there is another side to the canyon. If you are all fit and can hike for a day, walk down the East Portal Road. This is a steep, but paved, road that includes tight turns and great views. Talk about wildness. Ask why some people have devoted their lives to preserving wild places and wilderness. What makes the north side and south side different?

On the East Portal Road, you can fish, hike, picnic, splash in the water, and look for wildlife. But be sure to set a pace that's appropriate for both you and your grandchildren. When our son Matthew was 10, he hiked up the Grand Canyon and refused to stop because he heard it was easier to keep taking steps than to stop and start—you will have to decide your own strategy.

A word to the wise:

If you are campers, Black Canyon is a good place for you to share the night with your grandchildren. When we camped there, the animals in the morning and evening and the abundant stars in the dark night sky made it difficult to want to sleep. Hopefully the other campers will be quiet and respectful and remove bright lights—you should do the same. Did you know that the dark night sky is disappearing? The wonder we felt in seeing a sky filled with stars is becoming an endangered experience, so you should take opportunities like this to let your grandchildren understand the majesty of the universe.

Age of grandchild: 5 and up

Best season: All

Contact: 102 Elk Creek Gunnison, CO 81230 • (970) 641-2337 • www.nps.gov/blca

Also check out:

Curecanti National Recreation Area: www.nps.gov/cure

McInnis Canyons National Conservation Area: www.blm.gov/co/st/en/fo/mcnca.html

Red Rock Canyon, Colorado Springs: www.springsgov.com/page.asp?navid=788

Royal Gorge, Canon City: www.canoncitycolorado.com

Curecanti National Recreation Area

The Gunnison River may be best known at Black Canyon of the Gunnison National Park, but it is best accessed in Curecanti National Recreation Area. This is a spectacular combination of land and water that gets very little publicity outside the region, and it should be on the 'to-do' list for your family. Give it time and energy and enjoy exploring—just remember, this land is not for lightweights. Enjoying means getting out, walking, floating, boating, camping, fishing, and observing.

The river is set in a deep valley, but the recreation area begins in a landscape of mesas and ends in the narrowing gorge that will become the National Park. Three reservoirs fill this dry landscape and there is boating, windsurfing, and other water recreation. Fish in the waters for brown, rainbow, Mackinaw, and brook trout, as well as Kokanee salmon. If fishing is your pleasure, this is where to go.

For sightseeing, you can drive across the dam at the west end of Blue Mesa Reservoir near Lake Fork Visitor Center and continue west to Pioneer Point and Hermit's Rest. Here are hiking trails and overlooks that are difficult to match.

From Pioneer Point you can look into the deep and narrowing canyon and observe the unique Curecanti Needle formation, where Blue Creek joins the river, leaving a massive point of rock standing separate from the canyon walls. This is a steep overlook and you want to take extra precautions, even though there is a hand rail. From the parking lot you can walk both ways to take in the view. We suggest that you use this as a refreshment break. You can spend a lot of time absorbing all you can see from here. The drop into Curecanti Creek is deep, and the river has lots of undammed whitewater that adds to its beauty, and the peaks to the north include pinnacles and other beautiful formations.

You might also see bighorn sheep and elk along this driving route, so be sure to have someone watching for wildlife while you watch the road.

Bonding and bridging:

You can watch for bighorns and elk, find small chipmunks and lots of birds along trails in the park. The quest is the important thing. Being prepared, being observant, seeing, noting, and then identifying the animals involves a lot of learning skills and life skills. Wildlife observing is a non-lethal form of hunting and can help you forge the bond that hunters describe, if done well.

Keep a list, take photos, and take time to use the bird or mammal books to confirm your observations. The best hike is the 1.5 mile Neversink with a Great Blue Heron rookery and lots of streamside vegetation that attracts small birds. A more difficult trail, but fun because of the spectacular rock formations, is the Dillon Pinnacles Trail, which is 4 miles if you do it all. Mesa Creek is only 1.5 miles and has sheer walls that might have bighorn sheep, but the trail itself is moderate.

A word to the wise:

If you have visited the National Park, observed the river from Pioneer Peak and enjoyed the setting and the vistas, you must be ready to get on the water and see what the canyons look like from below. To get the best view, you can join a park ranger on a $1^1/2$ hour cruise on Morrow Point Reservoir. One warning—this boat requires a short hike with 232 stairs to reach the boat, so judge whether you are fit enough to do this. If you are, you can enjoy the half-mile walk along the old narrow gauge rail bed before reaching the boat dock—it is an all-around adventure for you and your grandchildren. Tour reservations are required (see website below) It is well worth it, as the boat moves beneath the constantly rising vertical landscape that makes the canyon so famous.

Age of grandchild: 6 and up

Best season: summer

Contact: 102 Elk Creek Gunnison, CO 81230 • (970) 641-2337 • www.nps.gov/cure

Also check out:

Gunnison Gorge National Conservation Area: www.co.blm.gov/ggnca

McInnis Canyons National Conservation Area: www.blm.gov/co/st/en/fo/mcnca.html

I've learned that when your newly born grandchild holds your little finger in his fist, that you're hooked for life. ANDY ROONEY

89

Glenwood Canyon Bike and Bath

The freeway takes a spectacular route through Glenwood Canyon, but the freeway is no way to truly grasp the magnificence of the route. This is a place for bicycles. The entire Glenwood Canyon ride is 16.2 miles long. Too long for your grandchildren you say? No. Too long for you, you ask? No. If you said yes, think again: if you take a shuttle and pedal back to Glenwood Springs almost every part is downhill.

Talk about maximizing your effort: let the bike roll, but not too fast, these are not hills, just the normal drop of a mountain stream. Like paddling a

boat downstream, this is pedaling with the flow, and there are outfitters in town that will provide you with good bikes, helmets, locks, and handlebar packs. You need to provide the camera, sunscreen, drinking water, and energy foods.

But don't be in a hurry. It's easy to feel like you are on the Tour de France and pedaling like Lance Armstrong since gravity is your ally on this trail, but to do that would only mean that you get less for your investment. Slow down and take in the scenery. Take photos. Stop at the four rest areas and use the picnic tables and the facilities. Take a walk on the Hanging Lake hiking trail if you are ambitious. Let the Canyon be a life experience and not a quick dash.

If your grandchildren are still too young to pedal this route, look into children's trailers or trailer bikes. There are many options that will help your grandchildren have a wonderful time with the appropriate level of challenge.

Then if that is not enough, or if you really do not want to do the entire trail, you can choose the downtown river trail which offers many opportunities to stop and visit the community, but still gives you the sound and pleasure of a river as your companion. And if you and your grandchildren are really bikers and want even more adventure and exercise than either of these two options, there are shuttles to more complex rides which can be arranged with the outfitters.

Bonding and bridging:

We all know that exercise is essential for our well-being and exercise does not come from sitting on a seat and burning gas or diesel, no matter how fun anyone might think it is. Exercise is the expenditure of personal energy, and just like your stove or furnace, it requires the consumption of calories—coal, electricity, and oil for them, food for us.

Talk about how important our bodies are, how we make the heart and lungs healthier when we exercise them and breathe in good air. Talk about how we fill our engines and what that means. There are foods that clog our arteries and damage our internal system, the same way that bad fuels harm our cars. Water is essential but so are those important foods that build muscles rather than fat. Cars need oil changes regularly because of the build-up of bad substances, but we cannot change our oil; we have to be more careful with what we put in. When they see you exercising they know you care about their health. Eat and live healthily together, so you can also live long together.

A word to the wise:

Ever have a day when a sauna or hot tub would be the most welcome relief you could think of? The cure for a good day biking is right here in Glenwood Springs—the Hot Springs Pool. Ever since the Ute people hung out here, people have known that the natural hot waters that flow out of the springs are good for you. The Utes called them Yampah—big medicine. By the 1890s the water was bottled and sold in Denver and on the Rio Grande railroad.

But drinking the water is not the same as bathing, playing, and swimming. Soaking is what people wanted. Now the pool is open to you; the natural 90-degree waters in the 405-foot long pool are wonderful relief. A warmer and smaller therapy pool is also available, as is a water slide for the grandchildren.

Age of grandchild: 5 and up

Best season: May–October

Contact:

Glenwood Canyon Bikes and Shuttles • (970) 945-8904; (800) 439-3043 • www.canyonbikes.com

Glenwood Springs • www.glenwoodchamber.com

Sunlight Mountain Ski and Bike Shop, 309 9th Street, Glenwood Springs, CO 81602 • (970) 945-9425 • www.sunlightmtn.com

The real mystery of life is not a problem to be solved, it is a reality to be experienced. J.J. Van der Leeuw

Colorado National Monument

The landscape of this monument will test your vocabulary—there are hardly enough adjectives to describe the breathtaking forms and formations in this accessible landscape. Whether it is the movement of sun shadows through deep rocky canyons, the haunting song of canyon wrens, the beauty of yellow and red flowers against a stark landscape, or the blue sky of the desert West, this is a place for inspiration and exercise. There are cliffs that rise from the road and others that drop off into valleys filled with rocks that look like sculpted monuments.

The land is part of the Uncompahgre uplift, a massive force of rocks that rises from the Grand Valley of the Colorado River and it is a perfect place for all generations to contemplate the power and age of the geologic landscape. The red rocks of the Monument are not only beautiful, but a reminder that the name of the state—"Colorado"—is a Spanish word meaning "red."

Enjoying this area means getting out of the car—it is a beautiful ride through the park, but locked in a car seat, your grandchildren are not going to have the same pleasure you do. The Park has a good visitor center that provides you with background information on interpretive hikes, trails and programs.

Bicycling is popular here and so is hiking. Photography, painting, writing and contemplative activities are excellent. But the most pleasure will come on hikes that help you discover the landscape that captivated the pioneer John Otto in the early 1900s. He settled in the canyon country and worked to make the area a national park. His dream came true in 1911 and now you are sharing in the heritage of this observant and caring man.

The Canyon Rim and Window Rock trails are short, easy, and unforgettable. You gain access from the back door of the Visitor Center and can get a wonderful perspective from a short walk. On the other side of the Center, the nature trail is a safe hike if you are concerned about the cliffs, and is a contrast if you want to see the mix of land, plants and vistas.

Bonding and bridging:

John Otto is an interesting person to imagine accompanying you on your walk. His name is in the brochures, the trail names, and in the Visitor Center, but he was not a politician or celebrity. He demonstrated how each of us can make a difference. You might ask what drives an individual to do good things?

Ask your grandchildren to try to imagine what he saw when he came here. Is there any place that is that special to either of you? How did this man affect the generations that followed him? Do you think he would be proud of the park?

Look at the birds, the plants, the trees, the sky, and the rocks. Close your eyes and try to imagine what you have just seen. How big is your list? Share your thoughts, then write a letter of thanks to Mr. Otto and tell him how much you enjoyed and what you saw. Your letter can go into your journal, or you can send it to the park.

A word to the wise:

Vertical cliffs provide unforgettable views, but this is wild land and there are few hand rails to guide you as you explore. This can be nerve-racking for the grandparent. The choice to come here depends on your ability to control and trust your grandchild.

While the trails on top are flat and therefore quite easy walking, the cliffs can take away some of the fun. If you are in good hiking shape you can start hikes from the bottom and after the initial rise, Monument Canyon Trail can be a nice walk; the towering rock formation will be quite impressive from below.

Age of grandchild: All

Best season: Spring and Fall

Contact: Fruita, CO 81521 • (970) 858-3617 • www.nps.gov/colm

Also check out:

Black Canyon of the Gunnison National Monument, Montrose: www.nps.gov/blca

Great Sand Dunes National Park: www.nps.gov/grsa

Mesa Verde National Park: www.nps.gov/meve

Rocky Mountain National Park, Estes Park: www.nps.gov/romo/index.htm

Dinosaur Journey Museum

In the shadow of Colorado National Monument and near the shores of the Colorado River lies a rich dinosaur heritage, one that is best explored at the Dinosaur Journey Museum in Fruita. This small museum is filled with dinosaur knowledge and if I am not mistaken, you might even hear a dinosaur roaring amid its exhibits.

This Museum is right in the midst of a land rich in dinosaur fossils and facts. There are four BLM trails—Dinosaur Hill, Fruita Paleontological Area, Riggs Hill and the Trail Through Time that are nearby and these are a good follow-up to the Museum if your grandchildren are interested and can handle more abstract ideas—that is seeing the land where the excavations took place, instead of mounts and models.

The Museum is a hands-on bonanza where robotic displays of dilophosaurus, stegosaurus, apatosaurus, triceratops, Utahraptor, and T-Rex move, roar, and come alive. There are real bones in the display and they are bigger than everything and everyone, including the grandparents!

Some you can touch, others you have to look at. This Museum mixes lots of imagery and science, making everything as accessible as possible. As you walk around the various dividers and encounter the different groups of dinosaurs, you might notice that there is an upper level as well. This is the room where scientists display their skills. Paleontologists clean and examine their fossils in front of the windows and you can see both the care that they take and the results of their work. If this is fascinating, you should then inquire about the possibility of visiting a dig site in Rabbit Valley—observing and perhaps digging for dinosaur bones.

For active engagement of young children there is a simulated dig within the Museum where they can shuffle through the sand to make their own discoveries while the older children will be fascinated by the earthquake simulator. There is also a river system (stream table) that can be manipulated and explored.

The tour ends in a small gift store and you will be happy to learn that they focus on objects that aid in learning. If your grandchild is really hooked, look for something that will reinforce the experience or help you with the next step in your discovery.

Bonding and bridging:

Colorado has adopted the stegosaurus as its official fossil, which is only right since it was first discovered and named near Morrison. A giant supersaurus was found near Delta and the oldest fossils were found near Glenwood. Almost half of all the flying dinosaurs are from western Colorado, while T-Rex and Triceratops are found in the eastern half of the state. And near Fruita and the Museum, Apatosaurus fossils were found (that's brontosaurus to us grandparents)—one of the largest dinosaurs to ever exist. Other adult dinosaurs in the area were the size of chickens.

This scientific inquiry has captured the imagination of young children for decades. Share the excitement and let the children amaze you with their ability to grasp the names of these massive animals, as well as recognizing them in the displays.

A word to the wise:

Sometimes a road trip is just a time to be strapped in the car seat, but one of the best road trips for dinosaur lovers is the Dinosaur Diamond Scenic Byway that brings in the best of western Colorado and eastern Utah. It is 512 miles, so choose what you have time for. Also remember that the Colorado portion of Dinosaur National Monument does not have dinosaurs to see and the Utah Visitor Center has been closed for an extended period. The Canyon Pintado National Historic District is an amazing area of pictographs, but that can be confusing for the grandchildren who have difficulty with the concept of time. Obviously there were no people alive when the dinosaurs lived: so while the pictographs are ancient, they are nowhere near as old as dinosaurs.

Age of grandchild: 4 to 12

Best season: All

Contact: 550 Jurassic Court, Fruita, CO • (970) 858-7282 • www.dinosaurjourney.org

Also check out:

Dinosaur Diamond National Scenic Byway: www.dinosaurdiamond.org

Dinosaur Resource Center, Woodland Park: www.rmdrc.com

Dinosaur trails of Fruita: www.co.blm.gov/mcnca/index.htm

Picketwire Canyon: www.sangres.com/nationalparks/dinosaur

Cross Orchards Historic Site and Western Colorado Museum

This is not an historic site where all the good things are behind plate glass: where the rule is no touch, no noise, no fun—this is history that invites you and your grandchildren to participate. In conjunction with the Museum of Western Colorado, this historic farm site once had 22,000 apple trees on 243

acres making it one of the largest apple orchards in western Colorado. Today, 24 acres remain and the apple trees no longer number in the thousands, but that does not lessen the significance of this Grand Junction farm.

With our reduced number of farms and our urbanized population, children are losing their connection with the source of our food. Orchards, farms, and ranches are no longer part of every family's experience. The weekend at your aunt and uncle's farm has been replaced by visits to the mall, so this is a natural opportunity for grandparents. While this is strange for the grandchildren, it is a reminder of the past for many grandparents.

When the farm is fully functioning there are costumed blacksmiths and woodworkers, farmers and orchardists, each engaged in their profession and each one willing to share their experience and their skill with you and your grandchildren.

Sometimes old fashioned cookies have just come out of the wood stove oven and they taste as good as they smell. Guides can take you through the original barn and packing house, the bunk house, and even the farmer's gazebo.

The collection of equipment and farm tools, old construction equipment, rail cars and even a depot let you understand the era and the resources that the farmer relied on. The main portion of the western Colorado museum is located downtown and provides additional historic background on the region through displays and exhibits. The indoor setting of the Museum allows you to see exhibits that would be out of place at the farm, but the farm puts things into a context where these exhibits make sense. The Museum also shows you the other professions of the region, the jobs that created the population that relied on farms for their food and survival.

In mid-October you can come for the Apple Jubilee and taste freshly pressed apple cider, crunch on an apple, or eat delicious apple desserts.

Bonding and bridging:

The Cross Orchard was prosperous until the introduction of the Coddling Moth to America. This insect—a moth, was brought in because of carelessness on the part of people.

Our ability to travel and ship things everywhere allows seeds, diseases, and pests to travel with us, just like the rats that came to America on ships. The Coddling Moth was introduced by European immigrants early in our country's history. This was not a malicious act and that is what you need to discuss. Sometimes simple actions can create great harm if we don't think about what we are doing. A harmful word about another person, a prank that damages property, a joke that hurts an animal or another person are all ways that even our grandchildren can do more harm than they realize.

A word to the wise:

A variety of beautiful fruits grow in the area and if you visit regularly you can sample as they ripen. It is fun to see the different colors and forms of fruit throughout the summer and into early fall. Pick them out with your grandchildren, take them home and wash them off, especially if they are not organically grown. Then taste them in a variety of ways. As we discuss in the section on cooking and baking together, this can be a really strong bonding experience and teach them great life skills. Work to expand their tastes and diet with healthy foods. The saying "an apple a day keeps the doctor away" still has some merit.

Age of grandchild: 3 to 12

Best season: late summer and fall when fruits ripen

Contact:

Cross Orchards, 3073 F Road, Grand Junction, CO 81504 • (970) 434-9814 • www.wcmuseum.org/crossorchards.htm

History Museum and Smith Tower, 5th Street and Ute Avenue, Grand Junction, CO 81504 • (970) 242-0971 • www.wcmuseum.org/crossorchards.htm

Also check out:

Alida's Fruits, Palisade: www.alidasfruits.com

The Farm at Lee Martinez, Fort Collins: http://fcgov.com/recreation/thefarm.php

High Country Orchards, Palisade: www.highcountryorchards.com

Grandchildren are God's way of compensating us for growing old. Mary H. Waldrip

Grand Mesa

Lesser known than the National Parks, and not as classic as the peaks of the Front Range, people often miss this amazing landmark and the pleasures you can find here. There is so much to do that it is hard to know whether to visit in winter or summer.

Grand Mesa is more than the classic mesa. Yes, it is flat across the top, but its sheer size and composition make the overused word—unique—fitting. Consider this—in a state where most of the lakes are reservoirs, the mesa has 300 lakes. The 18 natural lakes in the Mesa Lakes area are within walking

distance of each other and are the most popular. Here your grandchildren can learn what a real lake is. You can even observe all of the lakes from the Land O'Lakes overlook. This may not be the land of 10,000 lakes (Minnesota), but it sure looks like it could be. Check out the Grand Mesa Visitor Center and let them get you oriented for your visit.

Of course if you are looking for high country without the steep grades, this is the place to be. Here it is 10,000 feet high, but basically flat on top. You will still breathe hard, but not because you are climbing great heights. The high forest lakes and mountain meadows are available for walking, looking at beautiful flowers and birds, picnicking, and fishing.

Visit the Land's End Observatory too. From this historic ranger cabin you can see Utah to the west and the Gunnison River 5,000 feet below. View the peaks of the San Juan and La Sal mountains as well as Lone Cone above Norwood.

You will ascend 6,000 feet as you drive from the Plateau Creek's desert sandstone to the conifer lakes that sit on top of this ancient lava flow. Many people claim that this is the largest flat-topped mountain in the world and if it isn't, we are still waiting for someone else to make their claim.

Should you be lucky enough to be here in the winter, the Powderhorn Resort sits in an area that is blessed with over 250 inches of snow each winter. It has a great view of the city of Grand Junction, the orchards, Colorado National Monument, and the desert.

Bonding and bridging:

So much of what we do is in the summer and we lose perspective on the wonder and beauty of other seasons—especially winter. This winter landscape is inviting, although you still need to be prepared with tire chains in case of too much winter weather. Winter can be great fun, and simple things like snowballs and snowmen may be all you need. Snowshoes are easy to learn to use and if you play ball or tag you can laugh as you adjust.

The key is to understand conditions. Windchill is one of the greatest dangers, but you have to be careful of sun exposure, too. If a child is overexposed to UV rays, there is a real danger in later life. On the trail, the danger is dehydration. The combination of winter and high elevation makes it particularly important to drink a lot of water. Dress in layers. Allow the children to dress according to conditions.

A word to the wise:

The mountains are perfect for downhill skiing and Colorado is famous for all its options, from Powderhorn to Aspen to Breckenridge to Telluride. It is almost impossible to list all the great locations, runs, and resorts. But cross country skiing also has its backers. The exercise, the scenery, the feeling of independence, and the romance of the back country draw all ages, and grandparents who have enjoyed this sport have a perfect place to share it with the grandchildren. Steep runs both up and down are difficult for the beginners, so the flat top is a big advantage. This is an excellent place for a winter play day.

Age of grandchild: 5 and up

Best season: Winter and summer

Contact:

Grand Mesa Visitor Center, Grand Mesa Scenic and Historic Byway Welcome Center • www.grandmesabyway.org • (970) 856-4153

Grand Mesa, Uncompahgre and Gunnison National Forests: www.fs.fed.us/r2/gmug

Also check out:

Arapaho and Roosevelt National Forests: www.fs.fed.us/r2/arnf

Pike & San Isabel National Forests: www.fs.fed.us/r2/psicc

Rio Grande National Forest: www.fs.fed.us/r2/riogrande

A child needs a grandparent, anybody's grandparent, to grow a little more securely into an unfamiliar world. CHARLES AND ANN MORSE

Pioneer Town

In the midst of gold rushes, cowboys and rodeos, ski villages, and all the other reasons for moving to Colorado, there is the story of the pioneers. They were shop keepers, blacksmiths, newspapermen, school teachers and a variety of families hoping to find a home. They came along the famous trails like the Sante Fe and Overland trail and sometimes they just left those trails and made their way on the best route available. But life was not easy for them and we understand the challenge when we can visit a place like the Pioneer Village in Cedaredge.

Just south of Grand Mesa, this Pioneer Town is filled with buildings that capture the life on the frontier, like the general store with its wide assortment of goods. It might not match today's superstores, but many general stores had the motto "If you need it we will have it, if we don't have it, you don't need it." Ask your grandchildren if they would be satisfied with the goods in this store.

There is an old time printing shop, a saloon, a bank, the Marshall's office and his jail house. In the barber shop you can get your hair cut where the barber can also be your dentist. A mining museum is also located in the historic town and highlights a job that many had to turn to if the crops failed.

You and your grandchildren can stroll all these places along Main Street, but like most towns there was more than one street to explore. Wander around and see the blacksmith shop and the school house. See a homesteader cabin, the chapel and the depot. There is also a doll and toy house which will appeal to young grandchildren, an Indian museum and the famous Bar-I Silos that dominate the village, like ancient skyscrapers.

These buildings are either original pioneer structures that have been moved here or very carefully constructed replicas. You can wander on your own or get a guided visit. Knowing your grandchildren's patience level is important, because guides do not always capture the attention of the children and you do not want to spend time trying to get kids to behave. The important thing is to take your time and look and reflect. The town is the museum, and grandparents are the source of understanding.

Bonding and bridging:

We might not have lived in the pioneer days but we are more likely to know someone who did than our grandchildren. If that is not true, we at least lived in the age when westerns were common on television and "Little House on the Prairie" and similar series helped us understand the lives of our grandparents.

A place like this is full of images and memories, but we cannot expect our grandchildren to understand them if we do not take the time to explain and help them. Mike's college students can't even comprehend the mimeograph that he used early in his career. Illustrated books help make a connection between generations, but family albums are the best. We make these albums to share, so grab the old ones that your parents and grandparents made and use them to make the past relevant to a new generation.

A word to the wise:

In addition to Cedaredge, Centennial Village near Greeley is an outstanding place. Set in the high plains, this open landscape invited many settlers, but then challenged them with storms, droughts, and isolation. Scattered through the village are many homes that demonstrate that immigrants brought their national heritage with them. This includes the Swedish home or Stuga, and the adobe house of the Hispanic heritage.

Age of grandchild: 4 and up

Best season: summer

Contact:

Pioneer Town, Surface Creek Valley Historical Society, P.O. Box 906, Cedaredge, CO 81413 • (970) 856-7554 • www.cedaredgecolorado.com/index.asp?NID=61

Centennial Village, 714 8th Street, Greeley, CO 80631 • (970) 350-9220 • www.greeleygov.com/Museums/centennialvillage.aspx

Also check out:

Historical Village, Greeley:
www.greeleygov.com/Museums/centennialvillage.aspx

Overland Trail Museum, Sterling:
www.sterlingcolo.com/pages/dept/plr/vtour/overlandtrail.php

Santa Fe Trail: www.santafetrailscenicandhistoricbyway.org

If you don't know [your family's] history, then you don't know anything. You are a leaf that doesn't know it is part of a tree. Michael Crichton

Ute Indian Museum

One of the most famous chiefs in Colorado was the Ute leader Ouray. Today a town bears his name, but few people think about who he was and why he was prominent. A place to connect with the Ute Indians and this important historical person is at the Ute Indian Museum. It is a small museum, but worth visiting.

Located in the Uncompahgre River valley, this Museum is in the heart of the traditional Ute territory that was usurped by America in its western expansion. At one time the plants and animals of the river and grasslands provided food, shelter, clothing and the necessities of life of the Ute who moved from

grassland to high country with the rhythm of snows and melts, moving with the seasons, blending with their landscape and the shifting challenges of the region.

The Museum offers a wonderful collection of artifacts and dioramas that help explain who these people are and what their culture is. The clothing of any culture is important to understanding the people and how they see themselves—think of how we hold onto images of Swiss goat herders and Scottish highlanders. In this exhibit they have done a really nice display of the clothes, giving them the treatment we are used to for appreciating fashion. The paintings and the photographs connect the clothes and artifacts with real people. Explore these with your grandchildren, talk about the land you have traveled through, the names of states, cities, counties, rivers, natural areas that still echo Native Americans.

This is Ouray's homestead, the only land left to him and his wife, Chipeta. Chief Ouray Memorial Park surrounds the Museum and includes a monument to the chief and Chipeta's burial crypt. There is a native plant garden, museum store, art gallery, and a walkway down to the river.

Combining both natural history and native history is a pleasant way to spend a couple hours. Have a picnic, sit in the shade, watch and listen to the river. If you are making a road trip, this is an excellent wayside! Should you want more exercise, there is a link to a walking path that joins the citywide trail system.

Bonding and bridging:

Who are these people? The grounds include a memorial to a 1776 Spanish conquistador group that explored the area at the same time that the U.S. was becoming a nation on the east coast. This is a time to reflect on perspective—these people were here before we became the United States. Where were your ancestors at that time? What would your ancestors have thought if the Utes or any other tribe had landed on their shores and claimed their nation for themselves and told them that they were now the children of the great chief? Your grandchildren will grow up in a complex world where all nations are mixed in economics, politics, religions, and even sports. If every part of every nation feels even a slight sense of superiority, how will we treat people who are different from us?

A word to the wise:

Don't know who Chief Ouray is? Don't worry, most people who are not from here, or at least from earlier generations who lived here, will not know either. Born in 1833, Chief Ouray was fluent in Spanish, English and the Ute languages. Today he is revered as a great chief, but that might be because he had an "unwavering friendship" for the white man and tried his best to promote peace throughout his lifetime. In 1880 he visited President Hayes in Washington. D.C. and the president called him "the most intellectual man I've ever conversed with." He also met President Grant, but not every Ute was pleased with him; many called him a coward for his passiveness and unfortunately, each treaty he helped negotiate was broken by the U.S., especially after the discovery of gold.

Age of grandchild: 8 and up

Best season: Summer

Contact: 17253 Chipeta Road, Montrose, CO 81401 • (970) 249-3098 • www.coloradohistory.org/hist_sites/UteIndian/Ute_exhibits.htm

Virtual Tour • http://hewit.unco.edu/dohist/vftrips/utemusem/start.htm

Also check out:

Anasazi Heritage Center: www.blm.gov/co/st/en/fo/ahc.html

Cortez Cultural Center: www.cortezculturalcenter.org

Anasazi Heritage Center

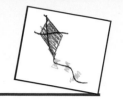

Sometimes after researching all the places you want to visit, you think you know what to expect. Then you arrive at your destination and are surprised. That's how this Center was for us; the beautiful building and great displays were a surprise and a delight.

An understanding of Native history, culture and lifestyles is difficult to obtain through books alone. The Museum helps bridge this knowledge gap and brings life to the many places you can explore in southwestern Colorado. Start with the movie theater. The film will help get you into the right frame of mind and ready to see historical exhibits within a living context.

Terminology can be confusing too. For instance, the terms "Anasazi" and "Puebloan" refer to the same people. The Museum explains the terms this way: "There never was an "Anasazi tribe", nor did anyone ever call themselves by that name. Anasazi is originally a Navajo word that archaeologists applied to people who farmed the Four Corners area before 1300 A.D."

The Anasazi Heritage Center provides public displays, and preserves artifacts and records from excavations on public lands in the Four Corners area. It is also the headquarters for Canyons of the Ancients National Monument. There are permanent exhibits on archaeology, local history, Native American cultures, plus special exhibits which often tie ancient and modern Native American history together.

The building is a Pueblo design and is very impressive. As you walk up, you notice the native plantings that usher you to the front door. Inside, the lighting and the exhibit design is inviting, but the hands-on and interactive aspects of the Museum will engage everyone. Try weaving on a loom, grind corn meal on a metate, and examine tiny traces of the past through microscopes. This is a rare museum because you can handle real artifacts.

A picnic area helps you enjoy your day and they invite you to explore the Dominquez and Escalante Pueblos (named after Spanish Friars) on the grounds of the Museum. These are an intermediate step between exploring the remote ruins of the Canyon of the Ancients and the Museum displays.

Bonding and bridging:

When you have finished at the Museum, take an expedition. The BLM sites are remote and can seem like a grand adventure for your grandchildren as you plan and prepare to investigate them. Start with a road map. Set a route and let your grandchildren give you directions.

The Lowry Pueblo, Sand Canyon Pueblo and Painted Hand Pueblo are three sites of great historical value and good places to visit with a camera and a journal or an art tablet. Let the grandchildren decide what is exciting and take the photos. Let them use or make a map to record the site where each photo was taken. The entire Canyon of the Ancients National Monument is remote BLM land with over 6,000 known sites! Any car can drive to Lowry and Sand Canyon, but Painted Hand requires high clearance vehicles. Sand Canyon trail is more scenic than archaeological, but it is a place where kids can romp and enjoy themselves.

A word to the wise:

While going to the remote sites can be exciting and rewarding, we do have to warn you that these are remote locations—usually without cell phone service. You are on your own. Take water, food, a compass and GPS, be prepared if you break down to put up a shelter—from the sun more than the rain or cold. There are rattlesnakes out there (but not that common), and there are many lizards and not to be feared. A lot of plants have thorns or sharp tips that can break off in the skin. Duct tape will pull off many spines if you do not wait too long. Use sunblock, wear hats, rest when you are getting uncomfortable.

Age of grandchild: 8 and up

Best season: If you are going out to see the ruins, try to avoid the heat of midsummer

Contact: 27501 Highway 184, Dolores, CO 81323 • (970) 882-5600 • www.blm.gov/co/st/en/fo/ahc.html

Also Check Out:

Cortez Cultural Center: www.cortezculturalcenter.org

Crow Canyon Archaeological Center www.crowcanyon.org

Manitou Cliff Dwellings www.cliffdwellingsmuseum.com

Ute Mountain Tribal Park: www.utemountainute.com/tribalpark.htm

Even now, I am not old. I never think of it, and yet I am a grandmother to eleven grandchildren. GRANDMA MOSES

Mesa Verde National Park

Mesa Verde, when translated from Spanish, means green table. Think of the early ancestral Puebloan people who lived here. What would a green flat topped table mean to them? It was the vegetation that gave the area its name and the vegetation that provided sustenance to a thriving culture that built some of the most enduring communities in North America.

This is not just a park, but a place for you and your grandchildren to observe the relationship of people to their environment, natural diversity and climate, and the survival of an advanced civilization. There are no knights and castles here, but until the late A.D. 1200s there was less conflict than with their European counterparts.

Ancestral Puebloans used the rocky escarpments and undercut cliffs to construct small villages with kivas (churches), granaries, apartments, alleys, and common areas that allowed people to share, communicate and prosper during around A.D. 550–1300 A.D. There are lessons here that you can share as you wait for the National Park Service ranger guides and follow trails into homes that have been vacant for centuries.

How did 60–90 people live in Spruce Tree House? What did they need to survive? How did the sun heat, the shadows cool, and the breezes refresh and cleanse their homes and buildings? A subterranean kiva stays around 50 degrees even on the hottest day of the year! Visit the Far View Visitor Center or the Chapin Mesa Archaeological Musuem for information about what there is to see and do at the park. If you are going to Cliff Palace, Balcony House, or Long House you have to get tickets at Far View Visitor Center. The Musuem offers exhibits that tell the story of the ancestral Puebloan people. A visit to one of the cliff dwellings is a must, but check distance and climbing. Balcony House requires the most agility with ladders and tunnels so it might not work for some grandparents. A drive around the mesa is long and should be planned for the best times—evening and morning when the wildlife is out. You will see wildflowers in the summer, birds in the open and easy to view, mule deer, ground squirrels, marmots, and even a bear or mountain lion. During the heat of the day your chance of seeing good wildlife is limited.

Bonding and bridging:

The people who lived here explored their land. They had to find their daily needs and inspiration from the land itself. The Mesa Verde has wonderful overlooks that let you view into the distance—even to other states. Some of these can be reached by car, so you can plan your sunset viewing accordingly.

Hike in the coolness of morning and evening. The best hike for mixed age walkers of all abilities is the Soda Canyon Overlook Trail, only 1.2 miles, round-trip. It begins north of the Balcony House parking lot and lets you walk the canyon edge (be cautious) through sage brush, yucca, oak and juniper. Enjoy views of archeological sites like Balcony House, as well as the natural beauty of Soda Canyon.

Another moderate trail hike is the Petroglyph Point Trail which is a 2.9-mile walk, and begins at the Spruce Tree House trail. It continues below the edge of the plateau to the only petroglyph panel that can be viewed from a park trail. Both Spruce and Navajo Canyons can be seen from this trail which is gated and requires registration. Use the trail guide to help you investigate what you see.

A word to the wise:

When planning a trip to a national park, or just thinking about it, you might want to use your computer to let your grandchildren read the *Junior Ranger Gazette* (www.juniorrangergazette.com). This newspaper started in 2006 and is changed annually. It is not about Mesa Verde or any one park; it focuses on the entire national park system and provides children with a wonderful way to explore the diversity of our national treasures.

Age of grandchild: 7 and up

Best season: Spring and Fall have the best temperatures, but summer is when all the sites are open to visit.

Contact: P.O. Box 8, Mesa Verde, CO 81330 • (970) 529-4465 • www.nps.gov/meve

Also check out:

Canyons of the Ancients National Monument: www.co.blm.gov/canm

Cortez Cultural Center: www.cortezculturalcenter.org

Ute Mountain Tribal Park: www.utemountainute.com/tribalpark.htm

My grandkids believe I'm the oldest thing in the world. And after two or three hours with them, I believe it, too. GENE PERRET

Hovenweep

In canyons of painted rocks and open landscapes of sparse vegetation, Hovenweep has an aura of remoteness unlike any of our National Monuments and would seem to be in an area where no past civilizations would prosper, but that is where you would be fooled. While Hovenweep is not huge like Mesa Verde, the small canyon is home to some of the most fascinating ancient Puebloan home sites still in existence in the American West.

The Monument protects six prehistoric villages along the Utah/Colorado border, but it is the one near the Visitor Center that you will explore and it has more than enough to fascinate you and your grandchildren. The walk is easy, although the sun can be devastating in this region if you aren't careful.

What really stimulates imagination and thought are the types of homes that were constructed here—there is a square tower that gives the Visitor Center group its name. The Puebloan people used to be known as the Anasazi—who built kivas (ceremonial structures). There are nearly thirty in the Square Tower group. The tower is perched on the Little Ruins Canyon rim like a lookout or the remains of a castle, but archeologists feel that they were more likely used for ceremonies.

Hovenweep Castle is another structure in this group, which means that the early archaeologists must have seen the same similarity with castles that you and your grandchildren will find. That connection actually helps the children connect with the village, since castles are common in children's literature. Dating to 500–1000 A.D., the European counterpart to these villages would have been the castles and cathedrals of the Medieval times.

These were agricultural people, a fact that is confirmed by their irrigation system and they were able to support a population of nearly 1,200 people with their methods. We might have a hard time matching that today. Visiting the Monument is a wonderful look back in time. The word Hovenweep was adopted in 1854 from a Ute word that meant "deserted valley."

Bonding and bridging:

While you look for the buildings and the unique way the land was incorporated into their structures, you should also look around at the life that might have been here when the Puebloans were still prospering. The most abundant animals at the monument are lizards, and the collared lizard is one of the most beautiful in North America. They like to absorb the sun, but they are smart enough to avoid the hottest sun and the cold nights.

Native people have watched animals for their wisdom and they have learned and adapted to the knowledge the 'animal people' have shared with them. Today we try to construct ways to work around nature—air conditioning for hot weather, heaters for cold, humidifiers for dry days, and dehumidifiers for wet air. Start with the lizard and see what other lessons you and your grandchildren can find, then observe the plants and the way that they grow. Are they different from the plants near your home? How do they handle the sun and lack of moisture? If you do not know the answers to these questions go to the Visitor Center where the rangers will be happy to help you understand.

A word to the wise:

The Hovenweep area is surrounded by wonderful sites. Those away from the Visitor Center are just a half mile or less away, so they are places to explore if you camp and give yourself time to learn more about the area. A wonderful way to bring the story to life is to visit the Lowry Pueblo, which has been stabilized to preserve 40 rooms, eight kivas, and a Great Kiva. This is part of the Canyons of the Ancients National Monument that surrounds Hovenweep, and is run by the BLM with over 6,000 ancient sites identified.

Age of grandchild: 8 and up

Best season: Spring and fall

Contact:

Hovenweep National Monument, McElmo Route, Cortez, CO 81321 • (970) 562-4282 • www.nps.gov/hove

Canyons of the Ancients National Monument, Anasazi Heritage Center • (970) 882-5600 • www.co.blm.gov/canm

Also check out:

Cortez Cultural Center: www.cortezculturalcenter.org

Biking Colorado

What a state! Climb, hike, drive, ride the railroad, fly, glide, balloon, dogsled, ski and bike. The options are amazing and bicycling is one of those sports that quickly brings generations together, but you need to be careful and take your grandchildren on trails, not roads. Exercise and fresh air, great scenery and a sense of accomplishment are essential elements to making a wonderful day.

The bicycle was invented in 1790 (yes it is older than us grandparents) by Comte Mede de Sivrac of France. The first one was like a scooter, but it was soon improved by a German, Karl Von Drais de Sauerbrun in 1818. It had two wheels and now a handle bar, but one thing was missing—the pedals! Kirkpatrick MacMillan of Scotland added the pedals, but for some reason the idea did not catch on. The Velocipede, with a larger front wheel was the new and improved model of 1860, with wooden and metal tires. In the 1880s, progress brought air filled rubber tires, and sprockets were the final elements. Of course, we now have road, cross, mountain, recumbent, tandem and a variety of other bike styles and shapes, but the important thing is not the purchase—it is the use of the bike.

AARP reflects on the value of biking for grandparents: "Bicycling gives you a low-impact, aerobic workout that strengthens your legs, including your knees. It also can help you lose pounds and stay a healthy weight." Biking is easier on the joints than running because it is a fluid motion without the compression and pounding. For children, biking is a way to connect to the outdoors, to give them valuable aerobic exercise, to prevent obesity, and to feel a sense of accomplishment.

Fortunately we have many bike trails to choose from that are safely removed from cars and other hazards. Like deciding to go for a paddle or a hike, you must consider your fitness, the weather, and the terrain. The terrain might even be the most important—hills are hard and if you are not in shape, they are frustrating. Check out the many Colorado options, especially those at state and National parks. Many communities like Fort Collins, Denver, Colorado Springs, Loveland, Aspen, Keystone, and Boulder have excellent paved trails safely away from vehicular traffic.

Bonding and bridging:

Your ambition needs to match the skill and endurance of your grandchildren. If you need more or less pedaling than they do, take a short ride with younger children and a longer ride with older kids, or, if they have more energy and endurance, pull over and allow your grandchildren to keep riding and challenge themselves. Pack a lunch, bring a camera, stop, relax. A trail is an adventure, so share your love of a silent sport, the satisfaction of using your own power to move, and a speed that allows you to observe and enjoy.

Keep track of your rides in a biking journal—miles, altitude, and favorite memories. Someday, they might return with their own grandchildren and it would be great if they could look back at their own experience.

A word to the wise:

There are some wonderful options for taking young children on a bike ride with you. We have an old fashioned "bugger" (trailer) that fastens to the seat stem and makes a carriage for the child—ours will hold two. They look backward as they ride. Now there are attachable seats very similar to the safety seats we use in our cars. They fasten to the handlebars and frame and the child is between your arms and facing forward as you pedal. A third option is a bike attachment (trailer bikes or tag-a-longs) with an extra wheel and seat behind your bike. This is like a tandem designed for smaller riders.

Age of grandchild: 3 and up with child carriers, 10 and up for extended rides

Best season: Spring and Fall

Also check out:

Bicycle Colorado: http://bicyclecolo.org

Bicycle links for Colorado; www.coloradolinks.net/Colorado_Bicycle.htm

Bike Paths; www.bikepaths.com

Colorado Department of Transportation bike maps; www.dot.state.co.us/BikePed/maps.htm

Front range trail maps: http://parks.state.co.us/Trails/ColoradoFrontRangeTrail/CFRTMaps

Glenwood Springs; www.glenwoodchamber.com

Bird Watching

No single activity between people and nature has so many participants as bird watching. No nature travel puts more money into the economy than bird watching. Nothing captures our love of nature, our love of flying, the beauty of wild animals, and the sense of the hunt, the way that bird watching does.

Some will argue with our statement about hunting, but we define bird watching as a type of hunting without killing. In this sense, most "hunters" we know enjoy the experience even when a shot is not fired and many we know sharpen their skills with binoculars as they add to their knowledge while observing and celebrating life.

Grandchildren love to play hide and seek, they enjoy the challenge of trying to solve riddles, they like action, and they love animals. Bird watching combines those elements into an activity that most grandparents can participate in and enjoy.

Colorado has magnificent ecological zones from prairie to tundra, and each one provides different food and habitat for animals. Mammals tend to come out at night, reptiles stay hidden and amphibians only appear for a short time and then are hard to find. But one animal group is active, colorful, loves to sing, and is seen in the air, where it is not camouflaged by vegetation—birds. Make sure your grandchildren see the variation between wet and dry habitats, forest and grassland. This sharpens their instincts for the natural world and for all types of wildlife study.

The Colorado Birding Trail is a great place to get your grandchildren started. The result of an effort by many individuals, organizations, and agencies to map out the bird life of the state, it provides you with hints about where to find them. Depending upon where you or your grandchild live, you can choose to discover the Eastern Plains, the Rocky Mountains, or Western Colorado as you search for the 400 species found here. Some birds come in winter, some migrate through and others nest in the summer, so it is a wonderful year-round and lifetime sport for grandparents and grandchildren.

Bonding and bridging:

If you like to play strategy games, you will love the
400 game, which starts with a list of 400 Colorado's
species and a bird book. First you look up and mark
each one with symbols for the seasons you might
find them in. Keep a list. Now, divide them by habitat:
Wetlands and dry land, hardwood and pine forests and
grassland, tundra and river valleys. A computer might help
with all your sorting, but you can do it by hand with graph paper or multiple
lists that you can mix and match.

With these lists you and your grandchildren can plan. What birds should we
look for in this season? How far do we have to go? Can we make trips that will
get more than one species? Which are common and which rare? To find out,
contact Colorado Rare Bird Alert: www.cfo-link.org/birding/rba.php.

A word to the wise:

Binoculars are the tool for this quest, but you must know how to use them
well. Practice looking at fence posts and still objects. Turn and focus. Be sure
the eyepieces are set to the right width for the grandchild and show them how
to focus. Make everything as easy and foolproof as possible. Start with birds
at the feeders, large birds in open areas, and refuges where birds concentrate.
And if you want to give them more help, consider the Rocky Mountain Bird
Observatory youth bird camps.

Age of grandchild: 8 and up

Best season: Spring

Also Check Out:

Audubon Colorado: www.audubon.org/chapter/co/co

Bird watching for kids: www.birdwatching.com/tips/kids_birding.html

Colorado birding trails: www.coloradobirdingtrail.com

Colorado Birding Society; e-mail: cobus@worldnet.att.net

Colorado Field Naturalists: www.cfo-link.org

Denver Audubon Society: www.denveraudubon.org/birds.htm

Rocky Mountain Bird Observatory, Brighton: www.rmbo.org/default.html

*One way to open your eyes is to ask yourself,
"What if I had never seen this before? What if
I knew I would never see it again?"* RACHEL CARSON

Cooking Together

Food comes from the grocery store! This is a common belief among a large portion of urban children who do not see farms regularly, who do not hunt, fish, or even cook! As grandparents, we have the opportunity to turn the kitchen into a science center. All types of cooking require reading (recipes), it involves math (measuring), and science (the interaction of compounds). So jump in, set aside the time, and start your grandchildren on a new path.

Cooking with your grandchildren will add memories of all sorts, in a very positive way. Depending upon their age, you can let them use a cookie cutter and decorate your creations, or you can engage them in measuring, mixing, baking, and of course eating.

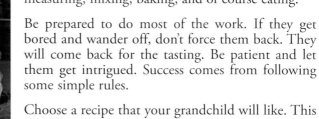

Be prepared to do most of the work. If they get bored and wander off, don't force them back. They will come back for the tasting. Be patient and let them get intrigued. Success comes from following some simple rules.

Choose a recipe that your grandchild will like. This should be a very simple recipe to begin with, but in one case, we chose complex and challenging recipes to teach a teenager who really wanted to learn. She was motivated by the challenge.

Start by washing hands. Cleanliness might be tough to achieve, but keep it in mind. Put an apron on everyone and if you can find chef's hat that fit them, the kids will feel even more grown up.

Set out the ingredients. When you invite them to cook with you, the last thing you want to do is make them wait while you sort out your cupboards. Set up three "stations" that keep the children away from sharp knives and hot pans. One is for mixing ingredients, the second is the oven or stove for cooking, and the third is the spot for decorating or serving the results. Use a stool if necessary, so that they are even with the counter and not stretching. Help them measure, but do it over a separate bowl so that extra ingredients do not fall into your final product.

For younger children, decorating is the most fun, although eating is always a favorite. In fact, dough may start disappearing before it gets to the oven. How can you beat an activity that is tactile, has great scents, looks good, and tastes great?

Bonding and bridging:

In our research we came upon a very significant statement—'build kids not cookies.' What a great perspective. This is all about sharing and creating. They are learning where food comes from, they are doing something that has a great outcome, and they are beginners. Don't think of doing this unless you are going to invest the time. Do not rush, or talk on the phone, or engage in other distractions. This is not a time for multi-tasking, but a time for concentration.

When the final products are done, especially with baked goods, there is the lesson of delayed gratification while you wait for your creation to cool before you eat. Think of some things you can do during this time—like cleaning up the area and dishes you used, and explain how preparing food often requires patience; we have to wait for fruit to ripen, for food to cook, and for the grill to heat before barbecuing. You might work on setting a nice place at the table and create a fun drink while you wait.

A word to the wise:

A good beginning exercise for young kids is making play dough. All you need is 7–8 cups of flour, 3 cups of salt, 3 tablespoons of cream of tartar, $^1/_4$ cup of vegetable oil, 4 cups of hot water, and some food coloring. Mix the first three—add oil and water and knead. Break up the dough into smaller units so you can make different colors when you knead. There are many things to do in a kitchen and it all begins with washing hands. After that you can parcel out the work—two year olds can scrub and tear, three year olds can mix and pour, and four and five year olds can learn to measure and beat.

Age of grandchild: 3 and up

Best season: Winter

Also check out:

Better Homes and Gardens cooking with kids: www.bhg.com/bhg/category.jhtml?categoryid=/templatedata/bhg/category/data/c_436.xml

National Network for Child Care:
www.nncc.org/Curriculum/fc46_cook.kids.html

The Prepared Pantry: www.preparedpantry.com/bakingwithkidsinfopage.htm

The Science of Cooking: www.exploratorium.edu/cooking/index.html

Young Chefs Academy: www.youngchefsacademy.com/pages/home.html

Dog Sledding

Living in Colorado means enjoying winter in the mountains. Why else live here? Snow in the high country is a source of both beauty and pleasure. And what could be better than a mix of snow, children and dogs? Dog sledding has a very long history and a very practical one. The first dog sledders didn't do it just for pleasure as we do; they did it because that was their transportation and a necessity.

Originally two breeds of dogs were used: Alaskan Malamutes and Siberian huskies. The Mahlemut Eskimos bred large freight-hauling dogs (Malamutes) capable of pulling very large loads over rugged country. The Siberian huskies

originated, as their name suggests, in Siberia. The Chukchi used these dogs for herding reindeer, as well as hauling loads. Dog sledding changed as the Gold Rush created a huge demand for dogs and any dog capable of pulling any load was harnessed and used until they dropped. It was the low point for all mushing, but it introduced the idea that many kinds of dogs could be harnessed.

Dog sled racing is a more recent phenomenon. The most famous race is the Iditarod held in Alaska each year. In Colorado there are a number of races, and in addition to running non-stop for great distances, many of these dogs are also racing at high elevations. One race, in the southwestern part of the state, is called the Mancos Mush. The town of Mancos makes the whole weekend a Festival so you can both revel in the excitement of the dogs and see art exhibits and other fun family activities. Watch the start and finish of the races, held on Saturday and Sunday. Try to be there for the harnessing, and all the energy that goes into holding the dogs back for the official start. Standing in the cold, surrounded by beautiful, enthusiastic animals and sleds driven by fur-coated mushers calling out commands, makes it feel like you've been transported to a different century.

It's great to get out and see the dogs and the mushers, but your grandchildren will benefit most by getting on the sled or standing on the runners and feeling the energy of the dogs and their power. After seeing the race, they will be supercharged and want to experience the sport themselves. A search for dog sledding in Colorado quickly yields websites on all aspects of the sport, including the ones listed in this section. There are many sites that offer dog sled rides of various lengths for a fee.

Bonding and bridging:

Kids, animals and grandparents—that's the big three! Mix in winter scenery, adventure and exercise and you have a wonderful experience that will not only give you great photos, but something to talk about with everyone else.

The lesson in this is the relationship we have with our animals. Whether we raise them for food, work, or for pleasure, animals deserve to be treated well. The old days of the whip and abuse should be a bad memory that never returns. Watching the mushers work with their dogs will inspire questions about what we ask animals to do for us. Is it fair? Are the animals happy? If so, how can we tell? Many children have pets of one sort or another and grandparents often do too. These activities give us a chance to talk about why these animals are important in our lives and whether we are providing them with the right amount of care and attention. How often does the dog get walked? Who cleans the cat's litter box?

A word to the wise:

Be sure to talk about your pets at home. The grandchildren will be ready to tie something to the dog and expect that the pet you have trained to lounge around the house will become a demon puller. This is dangerous for the dog and you need to share with your grandchildren the danger of putting something around the dog's neck. See how the harnesses work. There is no pressure on the throat.

Age of grandchild: All ages love the dogs, but for a dogsled ride they should be 3 years and older

Best season: Winter

Also check out:

Good Time Adventures, Summit County: www.goodtimesadventures.com/dogsled.htm

Mancos Mush: www.mancosmush.com

Nova Guides Inc.: www.novaguides.com/dogsled.htm

Winter Park Dogsled Rides: www.dogsledrides.com/winterpark

Now that I've reached the age where I need my children more than they need me, I really understand how grand it is to be a grandmother. MRS. MARGARET WHITLAM

Dude Ranches

We grandparents grew up with Westerns, the Saturday matinees or Saturday morning TV shows. Roy Rogers with Trigger and Dale Evans, Gunsmoke, Bonanza, My Friend Flicka, Sky King and Fury filled our imaginations with adventure, drama, intrigue, good guys and bad guys, and horses, always horses. It seems that all kids, even today, go through a "horse" stage when they admire these magnificent animals. Some of us never really outgrow this stage. I realized my dream of having my own horse at the age of 37, and for 18 years I lived that dream with three very special horses.

As children, those of us who grew up in urban areas had some access to riding stables or maybe relatives who still lived in the country and had horses we could pet and possibly ride. Today our grandchildren have far fewer opportunities to have this dream come true. One very special way to introduce grandkids to horses and some of the romance of the old Westerns is through a Dude Ranch vacation. We know this is always an expensive experience, but if you have the means and a grandchild who really loves horses and you have similar feelings or memories, then sharing a few days at a Dude Ranch could be the best time you'll spend together.

Colorado was once covered with working ranches and over time, as "dudes" (urbanites) sought an authentic ranch experience, some entrepreneurial ranchers saw a way to supplement their income by taking on guests to ride the range and live life temporarily as a "cowboy" or "cowgirl".

The Colorado Dude and Guest Ranch Association once had 689 members. But changing times, the cost of liability insurance, and demographics have reduced that number to 30 today. These are from the northern to the southern edge of the state, and you need to do some research before choosing one to make sure it accommodates people of all ages, with lots of activities geared to kids. Horseback riding should be the number one activity, but there are some Dude Ranches today that are more like full scale resorts and offer activities like rock climbing and mountain biking, which is not necessarily a bad thing for today's kids. A pool is also a highly prized amenity.

Bonding and bridging:

Animals can provide the best forms of therapy in the world. We can tell them our secrets and frustrations and dreams and they just listen. We can lavish attention on them, groom them, pet them and not need anything in return. At a Dude Ranch you and your grandchildren may each be assigned one horse to use during your stay and it will become "their" horse during this vacation. This is a good time to share with them stories of pets you had as a child and how special they were to you, how they helped your through difficult times. Learning to care for another living being, whether big or small, is an important life experience for your grandchildren. If you are unable to take your grandchildren to a Dude Ranch consider a visit to a riding stable where you can still share the experience of exploring the countryside on horseback, with a guide who might even look like a cowboy.

A word to the wise:

Horses are large and powerful animals and there is always a risk involved when we spend time on or around them. Cowboy hats are fine for wearing around the ranch, but when going out for a ride, make sure the kids are wearing riding helmets. Some ranches provide them, but others may not, so be prepared to bring your own. Talk to the children beforehand and daily about the need to exercise caution around the horses and to follow the wranglers' rules and instructions at all times.

Age of grandchild: 9 and older

Best season: Summer

Also check out:

Academy Riding Stable: www.arsriding.com

Colorado Dude Ranch Association: www.coloradoranch.com

Dude Ranchers' Association: www.duderanch.org

http://horseandtravel.com/ridingstables/colorado.html

Sombrero Ranches: www.sombrero.com

Colorado's State Parks

There are 43 state parks, plus 78 natural areas in Colorado, protecting 150 rare and threatened species. Each has a particular reason for existing, and a unique history, but they all belong to the people of the State and they are living museums of natural history, places of recreation, camping, hiking and boating.

Parks give you access to the wild lands that few people could afford to acquire for themselves and they dot the state with refuges for wildlife and plants. These surround us with the natural world and opportunities for renewal and reflection.

There are some locations that deserve special visits, but all the state parks form a connection for grandparents and grandchildren that is different than those found in city parks and zoos. Walking, picnicking, and exploring have a freedom inherent in the experience that really lets each person connect with a sense of place, experience, and landscape.

Rifle Falls is a good example of the beauty and diversity of activities that are part of the park experience. We took photos from the bottom of the falls, watched people painting, picnicking, and a couple planning a wedding. Then we walked the trail past the eroded bedrock formation where a grandmother and her grandchildren were exploring all the hidden resources. Later, we walked the path and bridgework above the divided falls, looking over, taking photos and watching the bird life.

Vega State Park is located in a high mountain meadow filled with wildflowers and a beautiful mountain lake; Yampa River gives access to a wild western river near Dinosaur National Park; Roxborough is close to Denver, but seems as remote as the moon, with red rock forming natural monuments; and Golden Gate Canyon is a 12,000-acre forest and meadow combination, filled with trails and only 30 miles from Denver. Many of the parks have lakes or reservoirs for boating and summer refreshment, while places like Eldorado Canyon cool you with the shade of steep sandstone canyons.

Yes, you can read about these things, but nothing beats an outdoors hands-on learning experience. Each park offers different options for hiking, biking, water sports, picnicking, and exploring. The challenge is to visit each one and find the unique characteristics that sets it apart from all the others.

Bonding and bridging:

What is better than making a new discovery? It does not have to be earth-shattering, just something that you have never seen before. Nature has many small details, changes with the seasons, changes with sun angles, and changes with migration and weather. People have always turned to the wild lands for inspiration, recreation, and information. This is still possible.

Together on a hike, on a picnic, or just watching the clouds float by, it is good to let your mind absorb the smells, sights, and sounds. Look for something you've never seen before. Something new to both of you and when you find it, put it in a journal, take a photograph, draw a picture. Capture that image and it will be a treasure that you share forever. It will be a—"do you remember when . . . " time and we can never have too many of those.

A word to the wise:

The state parks take time to explore. Keep a check list; give yourselves enough time to do something—walk, ski, bike, boat, fish. This is part of your heritage and like the National Forests and National Parks, this is your land. That means you can enjoy it, but you also must take care of it. Teach your grandchildren early about the value of such places and about responsibility. Pick up litter, pay your park fees and help maintain the parks. Collect photos and memories and then compose a nice letter to the park and tell them thanks. They get lots of complaints and they clean up and police the parks with little thanks; hearing their work is appreciated will mean a lot.

Age of grandchild: All

Best season: Spring for flowers and birds; summer for warmth, swimming, greenness; fall for colors; and winter for silence and lack of crowds.

Contact:

High Plains Region Office, 1313 Sherman Street, Suite 618, Denver, CO 80203 • (303) 866-3437

http://parks.state.co.us

Rocky Mountain Region Office, P.O. Box 700, Clifton, CO 81520 • (970) 434-6862

Southeast Region Office, 4255 Sinton Road, Colorado Springs, CO 80907 • (719) 227-5250

There is no other door to knowledge than the door Nature opens. And there is no truth but the truth we discover in Nature. Luther Burbank

Ethnic Festivals

If you are like us, a trip with your grandchildren to visit all the great cultures in the world is beyond your means; however, there is a way to explore the world if you participate in the ethnic festivals that dot the state. These festivals are really full of fun activities. Everyone speaks English, the money you need is American, and yet the people and the events pack enough enthusiasm and zest to help your grandchildren feel like you have taken a trip to a foreign land, and sometimes a different era.

A good place to start is with the Dragon Boat Festival in Denver, an event that continues to grow in popularity and excitement. The colorful boats are eye-catching and there is even a boat competition. Colors, designs and imagination dominate the vessels and captivate the kids. They also serve as an introduction to Asian culture and foods, the children's area, and the cultural booths.

Littleton is the site for the Irish Festival. This long-running, annual event is filled with bands and the Irish flags and colors, but the Irish dancers, often no older than your grandchildren, add music and motion that your grandchildren will love. For sport and energy you will not want to miss the National Sports of Ireland—hurling, camogie and Gaelic football. This is not like American football or international football (soccer). Be prepared for action the likes of which you have never seen.

Long's Peak is a famous 14,000 foot peak, but when it comes to ethnic celebrations it is the background for the Scottish/Irish festival after Labor Day each year. There are many adult events here, but the parade of tartans is a must; the bagpipes, plaids, and drums make this parade unforgettable. There is also a jousting tournament, which features real (not staged) jousting. Grandchildren also will enjoy the traditional dances, and they will love seeing the dogs that are indigenous to the Isles. These are just a little sample and the list on page 123 will help you find the ones that will appeal to your sense of fun and adventure. You can participate in Jewish festivals, Hula concerts, and American Indian powwows, and every one of them is a trip you can share with your grandchildren in both photos and memories.

Bonding and bridging:

You can choose a festival that focuses on your own ethnic background and investigate your own heritage. The foods, music, dance, costumes, and crafts make your own heritage come to life.

Take photos for an album. With all the materials that are now available for scrapbooking you can create a memory book that will feature the country, the sites, and the sounds and tastes you record. Gather comments and reactions. Taste new foods and describe both the taste and the reaction of your grandchildren. It will be great for the future.

You can buy cards and small items to add to the book as well. But the value will be in the discussion you have with your grandchildren about the variety of people, cultures, languages, foods, and festivals that make the world so special.

A word to the wise:

Your grandchildren might be wise about geography, but most Americans are not. Get a globe to see the planet as a three dimensional object and locate the countries that you visit in each festival. Add a flat map on the wall, and use push pins to mark it with your weekend travels. This kind of knowledge will serve your grandchildren well in school and it is an incentive for understanding both geography and cultures. It would add even more if you could get a music CD to listen to on the ride.

Age of grandchild: All

Contact:

Dragon Boat Festival, Denver:
www.csg-sponsorship.com/codragonboatfestival.html

Irish Festival, Littleton: www.coloradoirishfestival.org

Long's Peak Scottish Irish Fest, Estes Park: http://scotfest.com

Also check out:

Aloha Festival, Longmont: www.coloradoalohafest.com

Boulder International Festival: www.villageartscoalition.org/index.php

Boulder Jewish Festival: www.boulderjewishfestival.org

Denver Greek Festival: www.hacac.org/culture/grkfest.html

Friendship PowWow: www.denverartmuseum.org/home

Geocaching

Here is the ultimate treasure hunt—making your way through the forest and the wilderness to a desired cache (treasure), using GPS as your guide. A GPS unit is a complex handheld instrument that allows you to do difficult things easily: it can communicate with satellites, determines location through triangulation, telling you where you are, how to get where you want to go, and it even allows you to see the path you have traveled. It can tell you height and distance, travel speed, and even the time you rested. In short, it is your travel guide and recorder.

It does have its limits. When it cannot find satellites, it cannot find you. When there are too few satellites, its accuracy is compromised. This means that you must use your wits to find the location you are looking for, a small treasure that someone has hidden and challenged you to find using GPS. You should register to engage in this worldwide activity and then seek places nearby to start your adventures. Beware—this can be addictive. To start your adventure, go to the website or the park and get your coordinates. This is where geography comes in: the coordinates will be longitude and latitude designations (e.g. 45°N, 94°W), which in turn, are divided into degrees and minutes.

Study a map and find a starting point, then set the waypoint for the location you want and hit the 'go to' option to start the arrow pointing in the direction you want. The GPS only knows how to point straight at the destination; it does not understand that cliffs, lakes, rivers, and other obstacles require you to go around them. This is where the skills come in. Using a map, reading the terrain, determining time and distance, allow you to make smart and safe choices. This is why navigation is such an important skill.

This all began in 2000 when 24 satellites were made available to the world for position determination. As the geocaching website describes in the beginning, "Dave Ulmer, a computer consultant, wanted to test the accuracy of the GPS by hiding a navigational target in the woods. He called the idea the "Great American GPS Stash Hunt" and posted it on an internet GPS users' group. Now state parks and forests have joined in on the fun and most public land has something to discover; just be safe and enjoy the scenery while you hunt.

Bonding and bridging:

An activity like this requires planning and other participants. Look at maps, read about the place where you
are going. Study the weather. Decide how much time
you expect to be out and prepare for extra time.

Talk about the decisions you'll make. Whom should
you let know about your activity in case something goes
wrong? What should you tell them?

How should you prepare? What food and drink should you bring? How about
a first aid kit? Should you have a shelter in case something goes wrong? Do
you intend to split your group up? If so, should you have walkie-talkies? Will
a cell phone work in that area? What can you bring for the next person who
finds the cache? When you get out, you should record your adventure for your
own reference, but you can also go on to the Geocache website and share the
experience with others.

A word to the wise:

While it is easy to get excited about the GPS unit, it is important to teach the
basic skills too—how to use a map and compass. The GPS unit is wonderful,
but what if the clouds are too thick, the forest too dense, the rocks too close or
the batteries too old? When we know how to use a compass to find direction
and we know how to use a map to plan a route and find our way through the
landscape, we have basic life skills. The compass is a simple instrument, but
aligning it with a map is more difficult. Practice and prepare ahead of time.
Use a map when driving and let your grandchildren understand it and then
use a map when walking and let them see how to know where they are and
how to find their way back to the beginning.

Age of grandchild: 7 and up

Best season: Summer and fall

Contact: http://parks.state.co.us/Parks/StateForest/Geocaching

Also check out:

Colorado Geocaching: www.geocachingcolo.com

Geocaching for kids: http://geocaching4kids.com/index.asp

International website: www.geocaching.com

Grandparents Day

Ranking far below Mother's Day and Father's Day, this national holiday was first established in 1973 in West Virginia through the efforts of Marian McQuade, a mother of 15 from West Virginia who was as dedicated to the care of senior citizens as she was to children. In her efforts to reach out to the grandparent generation of her time, she formed the Forget-Me-Not Ambassadors to make sure that senior homes were visited regularly. In 1978, President Jimmy Carter recognized this effort and ushered in a National Day of Commemoration.

President Carter's statements at the signing of the new legislation included the following: "Whether they are our own or surrogate grandparents who

fill some of the gaps in our mobile society, our senior generation also provides our society a link to our national heritage and traditions."

The day did not get instant recognition, but there is hope that those of us in the Baby Boom generation will demand that this day be as venerated as the other days that honor parenting in all its forms.

It is the first Sunday after Labor Day each fall, a day sure to be overlooked since it comes right after the last big holiday of summer, at the beginning of school, autumn and family schedules. But don't allow it to be forgotten. Instead, make it a day that brings your grandchildren in to honor the grandparent's life. Your children can help make this happen, but it can be a success if you do the planning, too.

Grandparents do not need the things we used to want as presents. Most of us own all we will ever need, although things we can consume are welcome and if the grandchildren were to help bake a treat, that would make it even more special.

Bonding and bridging:

This day is not for going somewhere, nor for outside entertainment. Have a cake, have a celebration, but concentrate on the things that made your childhood special. The Baby Boomers are the last generation to have a childhood without computers, VCRs, DVDs, CDs, color television. We grew up with empty lots, cardboard boxes, board games, books, paper puzzles. Play some of the old board games—they are still around. Make a rocket ship out of a cardboard box (I bet you can remember doing that—thread spools attached to the box for controls, crayon scenes for windows). Gather everyone around and tell a story about your childhood, and make this a day of photo album reminiscence—but not too much—let them leave wanting to see more, not hoping that you don't find another album.

If you have saved any old clothing—a little dress-up can go a long way too. It might be good to pop some popcorn and gather around the old radio, too—if you were from the generation of radio drama, you can now order them on tape or CD. Turn off all but one lamp, sit on the floor and pull the easy chairs around the CD player. Have popcorn and lemonade and tune in to the old radio experience. Because we have put so much stimuli into our world, it takes a little effort to reduce the distractions and concentrate on the audio experience.

A word to the wise:

Grandparents lived in a world where there were a variety of sensory experiences. The smell of popcorn, the sound of radio, are part of the experience. But nothing is more nostalgic than the candy we ate as children. We have had a wonderful time getting boxes of old time candy to share. Kids say—"What is that?" and our contemporaries say—"I remember eating that . . ."

Age of grandchild: All ages

Best season: First Sunday after Labor Day

Contact: Your place or your children's home—this needs a home atmosphere.
• National Grandparents day: www.grandparents-day.com/sitemap.htm

Also check out:

Remember Mother's Day (May) and Father's Day (June), too.

For old time candy, try www.oldtimecandy.com, www.hometownfavorites.com/index_dyn.asp, or www.sweetnostalgia.com

Picnicking

"Let's have a picnic." Such a simple phrase, but it had so much meaning when I was growing up. It meant we were going to a park where I could explore, and it probably meant that we would be meeting my grandparents.

The picnic always meant packing food and dishes in a basket, bringing the charcoal, and a tablecloth. Why is a picnic tablecloth always a red checkered pattern? There would be a cooler for cold dishes and some soda pop. Then my grandmother would come with a hot dish wrapped in a dish towel. She had it wrapped almost like a turban—I still don't know how she did it, but even more surprising, that towel somehow managed to keep the dish and its contents hot for fifty miles!

This was a wonderful setting. We would greet, bring out the food and sit and eat in fresh air, surrounded by green plants and open space. It was a paradise of opportunity for an inner-city boy. After the food was leisurely consumed, it would be time to sit in a folding chair, or go for a short walk. Grandpa would usually accompany me on this stroll—"letting the food settle" was the code phrase for it.

Picnicking is one of the real simple pleasures that gets overlooked in this world of fast food, fast service, and a fast pace, but perhaps it is the antidote that is most needed. Spill something? So what? Get food on your clothing—no big deal. Leave the hang-ups from home at home. Relax. Eat with your fingers! Crack open the watermelon and spit out the seeds. Don't bring fast foods in their takeout bag to a picnic. A real picnic involves preparation and anticipation. It's a meal, time to roam, time to talk, maybe a swim, and then a revisit to the leftovers.

Wonder if there is a good picnic place nearby? Colorado has 43 State Parks, 11 National Parks and Monuments, and Denver has the largest city park system in the nation, with 205 parks in the city limits, plus an additional 20,000 acres of parks in the nearby mountains.

Bonding and bridging:

The old adage is that "the way to a man's heart is through his stomach," but perhaps we have to expand that to include just about everyone, especially our grandchildren. The picnic is about setting and comfort foods. Beans in a brown crock will always be good, but a picnic needs watermelon to make it perfect.

Let the grandchildren help with the planning and preparation. Do you cook brats, roast marshmallows, eat cold foods, or put a fire to the shish kabobs? Explore why you enjoy the food and why the same foods would not be as good at home.

A word to the wise:

Even the word picnic is unusual—it first was known as "pique-nique" in France and later—in the 1800s as picnic in England. Originally it was a gathering (potluck) like the family reunions we used to go to each summer.

In England, the Picnic Society formed for a short period. The group would gather with food from all the participants and no particular host. The German version is picknick. In 1989, the PanEuropean Picnic was a famous gathering and protest to reunify Germany. Through all these versions it remains: a way to gather large groups without having to open your house or cook all the food. What an excellent idea.

Age of grandchild: All

Best season: Spring, Summer, or Fall, but don't rule out a winter picnic, which can really be fun.

Also check out:

Bear Lake, Rocky Mountain National Park: www.thespiritoftherockies.net/spirit/Hikes/Bear%20Lake/BearLakeHike.html

Eldorado Canyon State Park: http://parks.state.co.us/Parks/eldoradocanyon

Genesee Park, Denver: www.denvergov.org/Mountain_Parks/MountainParks/MountainParks13/tabid/391205/Default.aspx

Have a fourteener picnic at Evans Lake on Mount Evans: www.denvergov.org/Mountain_Parks/MountainParks/MountainParks10/tabid/391202/Default.aspx

Picnic foods: www.fabulousfoods.com/holidays/picnic/picnic.html

The State Parks: http://parks.state.co.us

Colorado's National Forests and Grasslands

If you don't visit the ten National Forests and Grasslands in Colorado, you eliminate half the recreation options in the state. The National Parks are known for their scenery and services, but National Forests have a different freedom. We go to National Wildlife Refuges to find wildlife, what do we go to find in the National Forests—trees? Actually, trees are important for more than logs and lumber. They add to the beauty of the landscape. But you and your grandchildren should visit the forests for their grandeur, for the freedom to roam, for wild places. Here are a few special opportunities in this vast treasure-trove of land. In the San Juan National Forest you can explore the

Chimney Rock Archaeological Area with guided tours from May—September. Check their website out at: http://www.chimneyrockco.org/mainnew.htm.

This is a really important site in a natural setting that adds to your grandchildren's understanding of the Pueblo past. Arapaho National Forest has Arapaho National Recreation Area (ANRA) with five major lakes for boating and fishing, plus the headwaters of the Colorado River. It is a good place for grandchildren to begin to understand what watersheds are and how rivers grow as they move to the ocean. In the Arapaho you can also ride the Eagle Wind Chairlift to access seven trails, all named for Arapaho Indian elders.

Comanche National Grasslands includes Picketwire Canyon with one of the most amazing set of dinosaur tracks in the world. The Forest arranges for guided tours to this remote area. The Rio Grande National Forest in southwest Colorado is an amazing place to discover. Along the 236 miles of continental divide you can find the Sangre de Cristo Forest and then drop to the alpine desert. There are four wilderness areas that invite you to backpack if you have the health and conditioning to share this great form of travel with your grandchildren. But with all of that and more, it is the Wheeler Geologic Area that is the real hidden gem. Eroded volcanic tuff has left a land of hoodoos—strange shapes and exotic erosional features. It is not easy to get here. Check the website for directions and allow a lot of time for this special experience (http://www.sangres.com/features/wheelergeologic.htm)

Bonding and bridging:

It is hard to ignore the devastation of the Mountain Pine Beetle. This pest is changing the face of the mountain forests—turning the needles a rusty red before they fall off and the tree dies. Just the size of a grain of rice, these animals can bring down a large forest. The beetles lay their eggs under the bark of the trees and are transported to other areas in firewood. This is why we do not pick up and transport firewood. We do not want to be part of a problem. Help children understand how to be good stewards of the land. We humans have had a hand in the change. First we have eliminated the natural fires that used to be a natural way of creating forest succession and a way to control beetle numbers. Then we carelessly transported them from place to place.

A word to the wise:

The beetle infestation mentioned above was exacerbated by a drought that is more severe than we have had in centuries. Lately it seems climatic events have been getting more severe. Can you and your grandchildren talk about issues like this and think about ways you can work together to make things better in the future? You do not have to solve all the world's problems, but give your grandchildren the idea that they can make a difference and that they can help change things for the better.

Age of grandchild: 5 and up

Best season: Summer

Also check out:

Arapaho and Roosevelt National Forests: www.fs.fed.us/r2/arnf

Comanche National Grasslands and Picketwire Canyon: www.fs.fed.us/r2/psicc/coma/palo/index.shtml

http://www.chimneyrockco.org/mainnew.htm)

Medicine Bow-Routt National Forests: www.fs.fed.us/r2/mbr

Pike & San Isabel National Forests; www.fs.fed.us/r2/psicc

Rio Grande National Forest: www.fs.fed.us/r2/riogrande

San Juan National Forest: www.fs.fed.us/r2/sanjuan

Uncompahgre and Gunnison National Forests: www.fs.fed.us/r2/gmug

The closest friends I have made all through life have been people who also grew up close to a loved and living grandmother or grandfather. Margaret Mead

Fishing

A translucent line, a hook, a sinker, a worm, and a pole: what a simple list of ingredients for something that could change a life. Fishing is one of the most basic sports in the world and also one of the most popular. If there is water around, fishing is part of the scene. Of course, it is a multi-billion dollar industry, but fun is not based on what you spent, rather what you caught, and a sunny nibbling at the bait is a terrible tease, just as a small bass is an explosion of energy and excitement.

Grandparents need to keep the activity simple. You do not need massive boats and engines, a depth finder and a tackle box that you need a block and tackle to lift. Just get the basics and take your grandchildren to the lake

or the river. It is excitement and anticipation. Maybe it is even magic. Drop a worm in, pull a fish out or learn the art of moving an almost invisible string back and forth through the air, avoiding the trees and shrubs, and like magic, lay an elaborate "fly" on the water where you expect a hungry fish to be waiting.

It is the panfish you want to start with. They are simple, they are abundant in the right places and your grandchildren can experience success in a hurry. If you make them work for the big one, you are likely to see the excitement replaced with boredom. On the first fishing trip concentrate on their excitement, not the record lunker. Try for bluegills, which one fishing expert says are ounce for ounce, the toughest fighting fish on the planet. They are enthusiastic feeders, so all you have to do is locate them and they will be waiting in line to get on your hook. Spawning beds are in shallow water near reeds and the best rig is a bobber 15 to 18 inches above a small hook baited with a bit of worm on 4-to-6 lb. test line.

You will have to fight the temptation to grab the line and "let me show you". Does it matter if one gets away? Be patient. Isn't that one of fishing's lessons? Enjoy the setting and the excitement and then when you are done catching them, enjoy the bounty of your catch and eat them.

Bonding and bridging:

Catch and release is a wonderful concept to teach the children when they are young. This very simple idea encompasses sportsmanship and conservation and children need to understand it early. The idea is that catching is the enjoyment and there is no enjoyment if we harvest too many. We need to let the fish grow, reproduce, and keep the lake stocked. The idea of taking the limit—can be an exercise in greed if there are not enough hungry mouths to feed.

Talk about greed, about conservation, about limited resources and making choices about what we need and what we want. These are important topics. When you are having fun catching bluegills or see the beauty in the colorful trout, you have a perfect setting to explore the idea.

And talk about how the fish lives. What do they need? We need clean, pollution-free water, just as they do, but they cannot buy bottled water. To keep our sport a success and to protect the future, we have to protect our water.

A word to the wise:

Keep everything simple, the fish, the bait, the equipment. Don't travel too far, don't go out for too long, let the children have the fun, make their fun your enjoyment. If nothing is biting, move on. Add swimming, splashing, picnicking to the experience. Give them praise, not criticism. Help them to see the beauty of the lake, of the river, the setting, sounds, and feeling of being there. Do what is right—they will be watching you and this is the time to build the behavior you want to see in the future.

Age of grandchild: 3 and up

Best season: Spring and summer

Also check out:

101 places to take kids fishing: http://wildlife.state.co.us/Fishing/WhereToGo/101Places

Tips for fishing with kids: http://wildlife.state.co.us/Fishing/ResourcesTips/TipsforFishingwithKids/FishingTips.htm

wildlife.state.co.us/Fishing

www.aa-fishing.com/co/colorado-kids-fishing.html

www.coloradofishing.net

Few things are more delightful than grandchildren fighting over your lap. Doug Larson

Pow Wow

No one knows how Pow Wows began, although there are many theories. The word "Pow wow" is believed to be from the Narrganzeet Tribe, referring to a curing ceremony. Some think that Pow Wows were started by the war dances of the Ponca. The First Nation in Canada website says, "Songs and dances that signified spirituality and religion were used in ceremonies. Upon seeing these ceremonies, the early European explorers thought 'pow wow' was the whole dance, when it actually referred to healers and spiritual leaders by the Algonkian phrase Pau Wau."

I am filled with pleasure at a Pow Wow. Here I see happiness displayed in dance and music, conversation and action. Native costumes are worn as an expression of continuity and promise.

Pow Wows consist of social dances that have special meanings for the nations and their histories. From the very beginning, your grandchildren will be captivated. As the Grand Entry opens the Pow Wow, the eagle staff leads a flag procession of the tribal nation, the United States flag, the POW flag and military flags, which are carried with great reverence. The flags are followed by the dancers, first the men, then the women.

The intensity of a Pow Wow is unmatched. Your grandchildren will feel the drumbeat and may even get a sense of traveling back in time, as the music combines history, religion and social norms. The singers are important members of the American Indian society; the drums are sacred and passed on to each generation. Old songs are mixed with new songs, elders sit beside youth at the drums, and the dance includes participants of all ages and genders. Some feel that the drum is the heartbeat, an answer to the vibrations of the Creator's first thoughts, as the world was created.

Every part of the Pow Wow is done in a sacred circle that is inclusive and represents the circle of life. Veterans, elders, and organizers are all honored, and everyone is made to feel welcome. The rules are simple—no profanity, no drugs and alcohol, do not cut across the dance circle, and ask permission before taking photos. A Pow Wow is one experience that your grandchild and you will never forget.

Bonding and bridging:

The United States is known as the "melting pot" for good reason. Our country is made of diverse people from varying cultures with different backgrounds. However, others declare that we are more of a stew, a mix of cultures that stay separate although all contribute to the success of the nation. A Pow Wow is an excellent chance to expose your grandchildren to the traditions of the Native people of America. In Canada they are referred to as the First Nations. Here you can watch proud people celebrate their cultural identity.

Ask your grandchildren what they think identity is. Ask what traditions they celebrate. What are the special days and events that mark the year and tell about their family and home? It is also a time to remind them that like the people at the Pow Wow, we should celebrate all those who came before us and all life around us.

A word to the wise:

Here are some Pow Wows to put on your calendar:

April—Loveland

May—St. Ignacio

September—Delta, Pueblo, Hugo

October—Fort Collins

December—Colorado Springs

Attend with respect, some will invite you to dance and others reserve the dance for only indigenous people. This is their event and they must set the rules.

Age of grandchild: All

Best season: Summer and Fall

Also check out:

A listing for the state: www.fortnet.org/PowWow

Background, listing, and etiquette: www.ewebtribe.com/NACulture/powwows.htm

Bear Dance, Ute Nation, St. Ignacio: www.southern-ute.nsn.us/culture/powwow.html

Ute Museum, Montrose: www.coloradohistory.org/hist_sites/uteindian/ute_Indian.htm

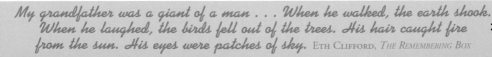

My grandfather was a giant of a man . . . When he walked, the earth shook. When he laughed, the birds fell out of the trees. His hair caught fire from the sun. His eyes were patches of sky. Eth Clifford, *The Remembering Box*

Old Time Railroad

No state presents more opportunities or more variety when it comes to stepping back into the era of the steam engine than Colorado. To some this is the land of skiing, to others it is mountain meadows, some see it as the cliff dwelling land of mesas, but to the railroad bluff this is Nirvana.

The romance of the railroad is hard to describe, but most grandfathers will remember their Lionel trains as one of their favorite toys and most grandparents can envision the massive locomotives spewing the white steam from their boilers at railroad crossings or moving along the landscape.

Trains may still rule Europe, but in America we need to look back to see a time when railroads dominated commerce and transportation. Have your grandchildren step aboard one of the lovingly cared-for trains, take a ride, and see the scenery as well as the past, and possibly the future of American travel.

Any railroad chapter has to include the most famous of the rides—the Silverton to Durango run. This is an all-day adventure that connects two picturesque western towns through one of the most dramatic mountain landscapes in the world. Ride the train through mountain meadows with snowy peaks against the skyline and step into the world of silver and gold mining between rides.

Another long and spectacular ride is the Royal Gorge Route out of Canon City. If Silverton-Durango takes you to the top of the world, this train plunges you into the depths of a dramatic canyon and along a beautiful river. You will literally be just a few feet from both cliff and stream and the scenery will hardly leave you with any time to do anything but gape in awe.

Should you have less time, but want to visit a beautiful mountain valley filled with mining history, catch the Leadville, Colorado and Southern Railroad for spectacular views that capture the wild history and landscape of mining boom times. Still looking for more options? Try the Rio Grande Scenic Railroad in southern Colorado and enjoy the Sangre de Cristo Mountains on the San Luis Express or connect with the narrow gauge Toltec Limited and arrange to be picked up by a horse-drawn wagon!

Bonding and bridging:

It's hard for children to realize how important rail-roads were in opening the West and in Colorado. Towns survived if the railroad came through and collapsed if it didn't. Even today towns worry about where roads, freeways, and airports are placed and how they will affect business. Think about the isolated miners in the mountain valleys. They may have found valuable rocks, but they would not get rich if they could not get the ore to where they could sell it.

Talk about the towns you know, where the new businesses are, and where the old ones were. What were the types of transportation that you had when you were the age of your grandchildren? And what about your grandparents— what did they use? My grandfather was born to horse and buggy but lived to see the moon landing.

A word to the wise:

A railroad ride is exciting as you approach and anticipate the ride, but once the train is moving it becomes the same as a bus or a van unless you help focus the children on the scenes going by. Bring some things to occupy the children if the romance of the adventure wears off, but also bring along binoculars to help them look. Many of these trains have special events like music and most have food. Children always enjoy the movement of the cars and being able to stand up and move around. Check the rides, the themes, the length of the ride and choose the one that will make your grandchildren the most excited. Better to have a short ride and a desire to do it again, than a long ride your grandchildren are not ready for.

Age of grandchild: 3 to 12

Best season: Summer

Contact:

Durango-Silverton Railroad, Durango, CO • (940) 247-2733; (888) 872-4607 • www.durangotrain.com

Georgetown Loop Railroad, P.O. Box 249, Georgetown, CO 80444 • (888) 456-6777 • www.georgetownlooprr.com

Royal Gorge Railroad, 1703 Fremont Dr, Canon City, CO 81212 • (888) 724-5748; (719) 276-4000 • www.royalgorgeroute.com

Amtrak

I have always loved riding trains, ever since my mom took my brother and me on a trip to Chicago when I was 8 years old. The sound of the wheels clacking on the rails, the rocking of the cars, as if on the ocean, made it an adventure of grand proportions, even though we were only traveling from Minneapolis. There was glamour (a dining car) and wonder (the dome car at night) on those trips.

Riding the train today is a very comfortable experience. The seats are twice as roomy as those in airplanes and you can get up and walk around whenever you like. There are fold down tables and even electrical outlets near the seats, so you

can plug in computers or other digital devices if you grow tired of watching the incredible scenery. The train takes us through backyards and industrial areas, past farmsteads and small towns. You can just barely hear the whistle in these well-insulated cars, but it blows whenever you cross over roads, and the warning arms are down. Have your grandchildren wave to the people who are standing by the side of the tracks or in their cars waiting for the train to pass.

In Colorado there is an opportunity to take one of the most scenic rides in the country. The California Zephyr travels between Chicago and San Francisco and stops at Denver's classic Union Station in the morning hours heading west and in late afternoon heading east. You can choose a 2 hour, 6 hour, or 8 hour trip. Two hours will get you to Winter Park, another half hour to Rocky Mountain National Park, six hours to Glenwood Springs, or eight hours to Grand Junction. You can take the train back to Denver later in the afternoon, or stay overnight in the town where you disembark.

Heading west, the train moves slowly upward through pine forests and rocky canyons, past rushing mountain streams, and around curves that let you see the engine up front. There are lots of tunnels on this trip, which children love, since it adds to the drama. As you near Winter Park, you will go through the 6.2-mile long Moffett Tunnel, the third longest in the North America. In ten minutes you will be through the tunnel and over the Continental Divide at an elevation of 9,239 feet

Bonding and bridging:

Plan your train trip with your grandkids. This means you need to look up information about the destination and find out what you can do in that town, before you catch the train back home. Planning for a journey is half the fun and builds anticipation for the trip. If you have a train set at home, set it up before or after the trip and relive the fun. If you want to start out on a smaller scale, take the grandkids on rides on the Denver Light Rail. These will feel like trains to the younger kids and you can make the trip as long or short as you like. And talk to the children about the way you traveled in the past and how it differs from today. Did your family have just one car? Did that seem sufficient? Ask them whether they think travel will be different in the future. Ask them whether they think trains should become a more important part of our overall transportation system in the future. Encourage them to use their imagination to project how they will travel in 30 years.

A word to the wise:

On this particular route, it is best to secure your seats in the Coach car (the left side is the one that will look at the mountainsides as you ascend, the right will look out onto Denver and the plains below). Then head to the Dome Car, since these are prime seats that disappear quickly. Pack snacks or sandwiches for your trip, in case you are delayed. The Dining Car and Lounge Car serve food, but it is more expensive than you may want to pay. Bring along games to play too, since this is a great setting for conversation and one-on-one competition. The Lounge Car has domed windows and nice tables that you can sit at for game playing.

Age of grandchild: 3 and up

Best season: Any, but summer will be the most crowded

Contact: (800) 872-7245 • www.amtrak.com

Also check out:

Cumbres and Toltec Scenic Railroad, Antonito: www.cumbrestoltec.com

Denver Light Rail: www.rtd-denver.com/LightRail

Georgetown Loop Railroad: www.georgetownlooprr.com

Sledding

Skiing has glamour, but for your young grandchildren, sledding gives them speed and simple fun without draining your wallet or going to much effort.

Sledding is a basic experience, fun that combines a simple formula—a sled, a child, snow and gravity. Of course the Olympics have included the sport on the grand and fast format of the luge, but your grandchildren have fun with the slightest slopes. One winter Mike just shoveled a six foot high pile of snow in our yard with a smooth path in front. The kids loved it. They ran back to the mound over and over—short quick slides, quick runs back and they had a full afternoon. It demonstrated to us how simple the activity could be.

Our job was to cheer, make sure they were safe and occasionally ride with them. Sleds were used for transportation and often were pulled by horses or people. This is another favorite for young children. When the grandparents pull them down the driveway or some other packed surface, small children find this as much fun as sliding downhill. Just make sure the surface is packed and flat or slightly downhill—we do have our limitations and a grandparent putting his back out (like Mike) does not make a good experience. If this is something you really want to do, look at a pulk. These are designed for pulling camping equipment on winter forays, but work well for your small grandchildren and protect you because they are designed with a waist belt that will reduce the stress. A good pulk will even let you cross-country ski with them.

The key to good sledding is a hill that is not too steep for the children, one that is not too exhausting for the return trip, and conditions that allow the children to play without danger of wind-chill. When children are moving fast, it is the equivalent of playing in a wind, and a wind increases the threat of frostbite. For sledding, wearing a face mask or scarf is important even on still days. It is up to us to monitor the conditions, avoid the dangers, and have some hot cocoa in a thermos or on a camp stove at the end of the experience.

Bonding and bridging:

Laughter is the height of bonding. We both ride down the hills with the grandchildren and when they were small, Mike would lay on the sled and they would lay on his back, making for a snowy laugh-filled journey.

The photos we took gave us a second set of laughs. Hot cocoa and a warm stove or fire, are simple pleasures that bond generations. We have used drifts from blowing, small inclines in city parks, and snow packed dirt roads around our home for these events.

A word to the wise:

Toboggans, runner sleds, plastic sleds, round disks, and tubes each have advantages and disadvantages. Toboggans can hold more passengers, but they can have crashes that involve people on people, and steering is difficult for younger children. Runner sleds are what most grandparents remember. They required packed surfaces, which might mean ice. They have a lot of speed, and young children may not understand the steering. Round disks have no steering so you have to have a really open area. Plastic sleds are getting better and better for general play, but do not steer well. Tubes are fun, but dangerous because they not only do not steer, they also bounce and if they hit a bump at high speed young children can be thrown and hurt. No matter which design you choose, make sure your young grandchildren wear a helmet for safety.

Age of grandchild: 2 and up

Best season: Winter

Contact:

Boulder, Scott Carpenter Park at the corner of Arapaho and 30th Street

Keystone, Silverthorne Recreation Center: http://silverthorne.org/recreation/rec_center.html

Littleton, located on the northwest corner of Kipling Parkway and KenKaryl Avenue

Ouray, Vinegar Hill • www.ouraycolorado.com/Sledding

Winter Park, Fraser Snow Tubing Hill : www.grand-county.com/sledding-and-tubing.html

Also check out:

General listings: www.sledriding.com/Colorado.html

Cabin Time

As kids get past the crib stage, they love any adventure that has them sleeping in a new place—motels, hotels, but nothing matches the unique flavor of a cabin adventure. The cabin is more than a room and a pool, it is also a place, whether high in the mountains, along a stream, or beside a lake—a cabin seems to put the family into a context of nature and history.

A cabin adventure includes moments of high energy and great drama. Grandparents must exercise creativity and flexibility with a blend of woods lore and simplicity. The cabin will be a place of creative imagination and fun, with lots to explore and new dimensions to test. This is inquiry, the highest form of learning and each new situation requires problem solving through cooperative thought and discussion.

The challenge for grandparents is how to both referee and encourage, while retaining control over safety. The first realization is the fact that a grandchild event is not going to satisfy adult needs, that is not the purpose. Take satisfaction in your interactions and observations and grab your rest when you can.

They need to become comfortable with the forest, beach, shore and insects, sounds, and settings that are not normal for them. When they get tired, as they will, little disputes become bigger and that is normally when grandparents are tired too, so be patient. Insects are always present and some sting and bite, but most do not. Let the little people meet the little creatures and go easy on the insecticides—those are human poisons too.

Grandparents will be exhausted at the end of the stay. Treat yourself to a couple quiet days afterward and give each other two hours off each day. Start with one night at someplace close. Choose a setting you love, find a place that refreshes your spirit, and let your grandchildren see what it is that comforts you. It is a wonderful gift to them that will give them a path for relaxation as they grow into adults and the demands of culture and economics.

Bonding and bridging:

Eliminate the batteries, the plugs, and the gimmicks. Take simple toys that must be maneuvered, that require creativity, and have the minimum chance of breaking. Bring out a few toys each day, something fresh and new, but not expensive. Let them have toys that can be outside and not ruined if left in the rain, or tragic if left behind. Playing outside makes the outside landscape more inviting.

You might want to bring books too, stories like Laura Ingalls Wilder, like *Henry Builds a Cabin*, by D. B. Johnson. Put the cabin into history and let them enjoy the sense of primitive and basic lifestyle. Share the stories of Abraham Lincoln growing up in a cabin, and the fact that presidents Jackson, Buchanan, Fillmore, and Garfield were also born in log cabins!

Let them cook with you, make things that they like, but that are nutritious and healthy, gather berries, and firewood if you need to use the wood stove for cool evenings. Enjoy simple games in the evening, a calm quiet without the sound, color and distraction of videos, a television.

A word to the wise:

There are lots of historic log buildings in Colorado. They are in ghost towns, historic villages, National Parks, and along the roadsides. Some are falling down while others are still homes and kept up with love. Talk about why we built log cabins and how important the forests are to providing shelter and substance. Do they know that wood sided houses also come from logs? Maybe a visit to a logging mill would be a good idea.

Age of grandchild: All

Best season: Summer

Also check out:

Colorado Cabin rentals: www.coloradodirectory.com/Index.Places.html

Dinosaur National Park—Josie Bassett Morris' cabin: www.nps.gov/dino/planyourvisit/placestogo.htm

Log Cabin activity page: www.cyberbee.com/henrybuilds

Rocky Mountain National Park historic buildings: www.nps.gov/romo/historyculture/historic_buildings.htm

Tenth Mountain Division Huts: www.huts.org

How beautifully the leaves grow old. How full of light and color are their last days. John Burroughs

Cemetery Visit

We know that this sounds a little morbid in the midst of all the adventures and discoveries that we recommend, but sometimes stories need to be told and facts need to be learned where grandparents are the best teachers.

You might visit a cemetery where a loved one is buried and begin a personal journey to find your past and your grandchildren's heritage. Seeing your family name on a tombstone has to raise questions about who is buried there, and why.

But in other instances the cemetery might transcend family and personal connections. That is how the "boot hill" of Glenwood Springs feels.

First, it is not a drive-up visit. You start from a city street and climb a trail that takes you above the rivers and the town, past mountain flowers and singing birds. It feels like a nature hike and in fact, nature will accompany you with feathers and flowers all through the visit.

Sitting high on the skyline, this pioneer graveyard is filled with a sense of the past and of course, it is legendary because of one grave—Doc Holliday's. Imagine a dentist being a western legend—try that out with your grandchildren. He was a gunfighter with tuberculosis who wandered the west in pain and frustration. Yes, he did practice as a dentist at times, but most often he was in the saloon or hanging out with other questionable characters like Wyatt Earp and Bat Masterson. This was the original gravesite for Kid Curry too, a member of the Wild Bunch who shot himself when surrounded.

It was neither friends nor family that brought the sick Doc to Glenwood Springs, but healthful springs and the hope that the hot waters would bring him relief. If they did, it was temporary and he ended his legend on this rocky overlook surrounded by unknown, but more worthy, people. Let your grandchildren understand that most of these people followed their dreams and lived out their lives like most of us.

Bonding and bridging:

Death is obviously represented in each tombstone and marker, and of course, each grandparent must recognize that if life goes as we hope, we will be the first close loved one that our grandchildren will mourn. You need not even bring it up. Eventually they will, just as one of our grandchildren did after his dog died.

In the cemetery you can let your children explore and see the symbols of hope, the words and the messages. Visit the oldest markers to acknowledge the pioneers and to establish the fact that history is made of all people and not just the famous. Gunslingers might make exciting stories to read, but the other people you see have worked to make a future. Make it okay to visit the cemetery, all right to talk about life and death, and let your grandchildren set the tone and ask the questions.

A word to the wise:

We tend to associate ghosts with cemeteries, so maybe it is natural to make visits to ghost towns a part of this story. Ghost towns are part of the Colorado landscape, places where hopes soared, disappointments rose, and efforts were abandoned. Are these monuments to dreams any different than cemeteries? When you visit one of these old towns or see a building aging in the fields, ask your grandchildren about the people who lived in those towns. Talk about the people who were in the cemetery and the various ways we leave a part of us behind.

Age of grandchild: 5 and up

Best Season: Summer

Contact: Pioneer Cemetery, Glenwood Springs, CO

Also check out:

Fort Collins Grandview Cemetery includes the remains of the original fort cemetery. Those remains were moved twice before ending up here.

Grandparents and grandchildren are God's gift to each other. Unknown

Library

Did you know that libraries are not an American invention or a creation of Mr. Carnegie? The Sumerians had a "House of Tablets."Imagine what it would have been like when everything was written on a clay tablet? The ancient Egyptians were the first to create a "House of Books" and they are credited with coming up with the form that would be the standard for books for the rest of civilization, even though books themselves changed over time.

A major development in books and the creation of libraries came much later. Your grandchildren should know about Andrew Carnegie, because he built 2,509 libraries between 1881 and 1917. His philanthropy occurred mostly in America, the British Isles and Canada. Open to the public, libraries have been one of the greatest successes for freedom of speech in the world. In Colorado there are still seventeen existing Carnegie libraries including Boulder, Fort Morgan, and Trinidad. Some like Littleton's have become homes to other businesses. Finding these old giants is like finding parts of the history of libraries.

All libraries are wonderful and offer great opportunities and treasures, but some also combine the excitement of an historic structure which means the library is a story in and of itself.

Many of these libraries have a special section for children and that is important to making your visit successful. These sections are colorful, often have small imaginative structures within them, stuffed animals, and of course appropriate books. It is good to go into one of these sections and sit and read a book with your grandchildren.

And, of course, if you are from the area and have a library card, the process of checking out a book is exciting and the idea of having to care for, enjoy, and return the book teaches responsibility. All in all, visiting a library with your grandchildren is a very good experience.

Bonding and bridging:

Even in the age of computers, books are still a reposi-
tory of knowledge, feelings, personal connection,
exchange between reader and writer. They are inti-
mate vehicles for knowledge that can be touched,
held, investigated. You can still see that intimacy
with your young grandchildren who are excited by
the storytime that libraries offer and the excitement
of opening a new book of words and pictures, or the comfort that comes with
opening one that they know and love.

A fundamental goal of libraries is to instill a lifelong love of reading and provide learning opportunities through books and various other media. Visiting
a library together can foster a special relationship between the generations
by bonding over the magic of a shared book. Grandparents have the patience
to allow the children time to browse, to look and touch many volumes before
making a choice, then bringing a book home to share. Perhaps the highlight
of a grandchild's visit is that calm period of reading just before bed. The book
is a magical bridge between you and the grandchildren, between wakefulness
and sleep and between generations.

A word to the wise:

Most libraries offer storytime when librarians read selected books. This is a
time when children share enthusiasm with one another. The readers use great
voices and sounds, incorporate music and often movement to interact with
the children, and the book becomes a magical device. It is important that you
are there with them. By being attentive and participating, you show them that
this wonderful experience is something you value too.

Age of grandchild: All

Best Season: Any Season, but winter really seems the best time to bury
oneself in the warmth and cozy atmosphere of a library.

Also check out:

A reference to all state libraries: www.librarysites.info/states/co.htm

Colorado libraries: www.publiclibraries.com/colorado.htm

Colorado State Library; www.cde.state.co.us/cdelib

Mamie Doud Eisenhower; www.ci.broomfield.co.us/library/index.shtml

Sterling Library: www.sterlingcolo.com/pages/dept/plr/library.php

Wilkinson Public Library, Telluride: www.telluridelibrary.org

*Children have never been very good at listening to their elders,
but they have never failed to imitate them.* James Baldwin

Waterfalls

If water and rocks are two of the basic elements of childhood creativity, a waterfall has to be artistic extension of our basic inspiration. The tumbling of waters over a rock face, the white patterns, and the soothing sound, all make for a wonderful opportunity to take photos, draw, play in the water and generally enjoy the wonder of nature. It is not surprising that the Ojibwe (Chippewa) heard Manitou—the 'great mystery' or 'spirit' in the tumbling waters. It was a voice of the land itself combining the resonance of land and water.

Waterfalls are abundant in mountainous Colorado, tumbling off the ice and snow covered peaks. There are lists and local attractions that talk about waterfalls, but we do not believe that anyone really knows how many there are in the state, although they claim to have more than anyone else. Each mountain literally bleeds waterfalls!

There are some waterfalls that everyone visits, like the famous Seven Falls in Colorado Springs. This seven step waterfalls cascades over granite and you can ride an elevator to get a bird's eye view of the drop. Box Canyon Falls at Ouray is another place with a charge and it is worth it. This 285-foot falls is from a small stream that flows through a series of dark rock rooms to form a box canyon. The walkway allows you wonderful views of this energy filled flow and your grandchildren will love the feel of the cool mist. Box Canyon Falls exits into an Important Bird Area, according to the National Audubon Society. At the feeders near the entrance, your grandchildren will love to watch the colorful birds and small mammals.

Boulder Falls in Boulder Canyon near the city of Boulder is also popular and deserves to be. Some call it the Yosemite of Colorado, but we are not ready to give it that much fame. A tungsten mine once threatened the 70-foot Boulder Falls but a philanthropist donated the land and saved it for all generations. Judd Falls near Gothic requires an easy two mile hike and gives you a nice remote feeling. But be careful here, there are no hand rails to protect you. This brief list has to include North Clear Creek Falls near Lake City in the San Juans which has made at least one list of the top ten waterfalls in the U.S.

Bonding and bridging:

We can share many things with our grandchildren, but the sense of discovery marks our movement through life, as well as the journey of history. Try not to tell them what they will see, and when you get there, let them voice their opinions before you give them yours. Don't tell your grandchildren what will be at the end of the trail, let them find out; in fact, let them show you.

If you know there is a waterfall, that is fine, but a "let's see what we can find" approach creates greater excitement and encourages discovering. The children will try to show you discoveries as you go, and then when the waterfall appears they will be so pleased to say, "Look Grand . . . a waterfall!" Talk about how important water is and how we have to take care of it. Let them see the waterfalls as a symbol for quality of life.

A word to the wise:

As gorgeous as these waterfalls are, you should provide your grandchild with access to a small stream where the drops are only inches and the flow is gentle. Let them float sticks, boats, corks and see them swirl and whirl in the white foam. This is a science lesson, a lesson for future paddlers, and one of the most engaging activities you can do. Our grandson Matthew played for hours in a small creek behind his great-grandmother's home. We moved rocks, floated sticks, and created worlds that were just right for his five year old mind. The large falls inspire and they love the spray and the rainbows, but the little ones engage them.

Age of grandchild: All

Best Season: Spring for the big flows, summer for gentler waters where you can find some places to play.

Also check out:

Box Canyon Falls, Ouray: www.ouraycolorado.com/boxcanyon

Rifle State Park: http://parks.state.co.us/Parks/riflefalls

Rocky Mountain National Park: www.nps.gov/romo/index.htm

Seven Falls: www.sevenfalls.com/home/index.cfm

Waterfalls to hike to:
www.colorado-hiking-vacations.com/colorado-waterfalls.html

The fire is the main comfort of the camp, whether in summer or winter and is about as ample at one season as at another. It is as well for cheerfulness as for warmth and dryness. HENRY DAVID THOREAU

Celebrate Winter

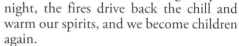

Let those Floridians bask on the beaches in their skimpy clothing; in the mountains we celebrate snow! Bundled up in clothes that definitely lack the body sculpting of bikinis and Speedos—winter celebrations are about rosy cheeks, breath you can see, caps that make hair appointments worthless, and warm clothes that make everyone look like penguins in Technicolor.

Sleigh rides and snowballs, snowmen and St. Nicholas, hot cider, hot cocoa, and warm fires are the ingredients. We know how to laugh at the cold, frolic in the whiteness and slip and slide with laughter. This is the land of skis, snowshoes, and slippery roads. The snow reflects the moon and lights up the

night, the fires drive back the chill and warm our spirits, and we become children again.

In Breckenridge they give thanks to the mythical god of snow—Ullr with hijinks that includes a parade, live music, ice skating and, of course, skiing. Bear Creek Nature Center in Colorado Springs celebrates a winter's trail day with snowshoes and cross country skis. In Ouray, the Ice Festival marks the beginning of their ice-climbing season and opens their ice park—here are some exciting events that older grandchildren can participate in and the visual images are spectacular. Aspen has Wintersköl, a celebration of alpine lifestyle with snow sculptures, ice carving, fireworks and skiing. Food, dog fashions and fun are all part of the Wintersköl celebration.

Canon City, gateway to Royal Gorge, holds Sleigh Bell Celebration, a December holiday festival filled with lights, carols, and even train rides. Ice Sculptures, roasted chestnuts, and hot cocoa are part of this event that features lots of costumed characters and family fun.

Durango has Snowdown, which has entertained the community and visitors for over 30 years. Based on an insult to the way the people of Durango dress, they have responded to the insult for over three decades and will continue as long as there is laughter in the town. The highlight is the Friday night parade. Many communities have winter solstice parties, where a bonfire helps burn away the long winter night and encourages the sun to return and warm the days—but not too much. Winter is too much fun to want it to go away.

Bonding and bridging:

Grandparents experienced a time of simpler games and entertainments. We found our fun in snow drifts and piles of leaves, and trying to catch snowflakes on our tongues. Ours was not a simpler time, but a time of different pressures and entertainments. Who among us does not like to talk about "when we were young..." But there is value in this. The winters were different and the only way for the children to understand is to share stories and have common experiences. Runner sleds are harder to find, the old shoddy ice skates with no support for our ankles have been replaced with space age plastic skates. Outdoor rinks have gone indoors; ice fishing has entire cabin complexes with TV and couch, stoves and furnaces. Our task is to bring back the simplicity of the experience.

A word to the wise:

I am sorry to say—we do not bend, bounce, and slide with the same grace as we did when we were the ages of our grandchildren. A grandparent lying on the ice in pain is not good. Get boots with grip, dress appropriately even if it is not always flattering and show your grandchildren your wisdom, rather than your fragility. This goes for driving too. Reaction time is not something we can get back by strength of will. We need to think about that when we drive and how we drive. In the morning the roads are slick with the chill and the exhaust of cars, but if we wait until the sun shines on the blacktop we can apply solar heating to our safety. Make winter celebrations something you can do each year, because you make wise decisions each year.

Age of grandchild: All

Best season: Winter

Websites:

Breckenridge: www.gobreck.com

Colorado festivals: www.Colorado.com

Durango: www.snowdown.org

Ouray Ice Festival: www.ourayicefestival.com

Sleigh Bell Celebration:
www.cdwebmaker.com/festiville/SBC/sleighbellcelebration.shtml

Index

About the Authors

Mike Link:

Mike Link is the author of 22 books and numerous magazine articles. He and his wife Kate live in Willow River, Minnesota where they enjoy having their grandchildren discover the world of nature and play. The bird feeders are always full and the forest has wonderful trails.

For 37 years Mike directed the Audubon Center and now entering retirement, he is looking forward to writing, teaching for both Northland College and Hamline University, and of course spending time with the grandchildren.

As his books attest, traveling is another passion. With fifty states and twenty countries covering his travels, paddles, hikes, and explorations, he feels that he owes a debt to the earth. Whether we call it Mother Nature, Gaia, or Creation, the earth is our source of air, water and sustenance and its destruction is a crime.

Their son Jon has continued to carry the family outdoor tradition into the wilds of Alaska as a kayak ranger with his wife Kristin. Daughter Julie works for Best Buy in St. Paul and raises grandson Matthew. Mike's son Matt died in a kayak accident in New Zealand and little Matthew is a spirited tribute to his uncle. Alyssa has her hands full with twins Aren and Ryan and little Annalise, while husband Troy is deployed in Afghanistan.

Kate Crowley:

Since marrying Mike and moving to the country twenty-two years ago, she has been surrounded by forests, prairies, birds, dogs, cats, horses and lots of other wild creatures. When Mike built her Lady Slipper Cottage in the woods, her dream expanded, but it wasn't complete until she became a grandmother.

Kate has been a naturalist, an educator, and a writer for 30 years, first at the Minnesota Zoo and the Audubon Center of the North Woods. She has co-authored 12 books with Mike and writes for magazines and a monthly nature newspaper column. Kate enjoys hiking, biking, skiing, scrapbooking, reading and spending as much time as possible with her grandchildren. She cares deeply about preserving the natural world.

Visit Mike and Kate's website at www.GrandparentsAmericanStyle.com

Notes

Date:

Comments:

Notes

Date:

Comments:

Notes

Date:

Comments: